Overthinking, Obsessing, and Overanalyzing

A Comprehensive Guide to Understanding, Managing, and Overcoming Intrusive Thoughts and Obsessive-Compulsive Disorder (OCD)

Richard Banks

© Copyright 2023 by Richard Banks. All right reserved

The content contained within this book may not be reproduced, duplicated or transmitted without direct written permission from the author or the publisher.

Under no circumstances will any blame or legal responsibility be held against the publisher, or author, for any damages, reparation, or monetary loss due to the information contained within this book. Either directly or indirectly.

Legal Notice:

This book is copyright protected. This book is only for personal use. You cannot amend, distribute, sell, use, quote or paraphrase any part, or the content within this book, without the consent of the author or publisher.

Disclaimer Notice:

Please note the information contained within this document is for educational and entertainment purposes only. All effort has been executed to present accurate, up to date, and reliable, complete information. No warranties of any kind are declared or implied. Readers acknowledge that the author is not engaging in the rendering of legal, financial, medical or professional advice. The content within this book has been derived from various sources. Please consult a licensed professional before attempting any techniques outlined in this book.

By reading this document, the reader agrees that under no circumstances is the author responsible for any losses, direct or indirect, which are incurred as a result of the use of the information contained within this document, including, but not limited to, — errors, omissions, or inaccuracies.

Why You Should Read This Book

Do you find yourself trapped in a cycle of negative thoughts? Are you struggling to let go of worries and concerns, even when they're no longer productive? Do you feel like your thoughts and actions are beyond your control? Do you struggle with obsessive thoughts and compulsive behaviors? If so, you're not alone.

Introducing *Overthinking, Obsessing, and Overanalyzing*, a book that can help you understand and manage OCD and overthinking. This book will help you understand what OCD is and how it affects people. But that's not all! In this comprehensive guide, you'll learn how to break free from overthinking and take back control of your thoughts.

The book begins by defining overthinking and its

impact on mental health and overall well-being. It then delves into the different types of overthinking and their causes, exploring the relationship between overthinking and anxiety, depression, and other mental health conditions.

Once you have a deeper understanding of overthinking, the book examines the impact of overthinking on various aspects of life, including work, relationships, and overall happiness. It provides examples and case studies to illustrate the point.

This book will teach you about different resources available to help manage your symptoms, including self-help techniques, mindfulness-based interventions, and organizational and time-management strategies. You'll also learn about different medications and therapies used to treat OCD.

Don't let OCD and overthinking control your life

any longer. This book can help you take the first step towards managing your symptoms and feeling in control again. It's an easy-to-read guide that will help you understand your condition and give you the tools to manage it.

This book will help you:

- Understand the definition and impact of overthinking on mental health and overall well-being
- Understand what OCD is and how it affects people
- Understand the connection between overthinking and mental health conditions such as anxiety, depression, and PTSD
- Learn strategies for managing symptoms
- Learn about medications and therapies used to treat OCD
- Learn about mindfulness-based interventions

- Learn about organizational and time-management strategies
- Learn about supporting loved ones with OCD

Don't wait any longer! Order your copy of *Overthinking, Obsessing, and Overanalyzing* today and take the first step towards managing your symptoms and feeling in control again.

Thank You!

Thank you for your purchase.

I am dedicated to making the most enriching and informational content. I hope it meets your expectations and you gain a lot from it.

Your comments and feedback are important to me because they help me to provide the best material possible. So, if you have any questions or concerns, please email me at richardbanks.books@gmail.com.

Again, thank you for your purchase.

Overthinking, Obsessing, and Overanalyzing

Introduction 13

Chapter 1: The Prevalence and Impact of OCD 23

What Is OCD? 23

Historical Overview of OCD 25

Current Diagnostic Guidelines of OCD 28

OCD Prevalence 29

OCD Impact 33

Chapter 2: Understanding OCD 41

Obsessions 43

Compulsions 45

Relationship between Obsession and Compulsion 48

Subtypes of OCD 50

Some Common Conditions Mistaken for OCD 54

Theories of Causes of OCD 59

Are You Simply Obsessive or Do You Have Obsessive-compulsive Disorder? 64

Chapter 3: Coping with OCD 69

The Impact of OCD on Daily Life 69

Strategies for Managing Symptoms 73

Self-help Techniques and Coping Skills 78

Mindfulness-based Interventions and Stress Management Techniques 79

ORGANIZATIONAL AND TIME-MANAGEMENT STRATEGIES 82

SUPPORT RESOURCES 84

MEDICATIONS USED TO TREAT OCD 87

BEHAVIORAL AND COGNITIVE THERAPIES 88

THE ROLE OF PSYCHOANALYTIC APPROACHES IN THE TREATMENT OF OCD 91

OBJECT RELATIONS THEORY AND ITS CRITICISMS 94

COMBINATION THERAPY AND TREATMENT RESISTANCE 96

FUTURE RESEARCH IN OCD 98

CHAPTER 4: OVERTHINKING AND OCD 103

RUMINATION 104

WORRY 104

CATASTROPHIZING 105

INTRUSIVE THOUGHTS 106

INTRUSIVE THOUGHTS VS. OCD THOUGHTS 106

WHAT ARE THE DIFFERENT FACTORS THAT MAY CONTRIBUTE TO OVERTHINKING? 108

IMPACT OF OVERTHINKING 110

NEGATIVE EFFECTS OF OVERTHINKING 113

OVERTHINKING CASE STUDIES 115

THE CONNECTION BETWEEN OVERTHINKING AND OCD 117

Difference between Overthinking and OCD 118

Chapter 5: The Neural Basis of Overthinking 123

Brain and Overthinking 123

Neurotransmitters and Overthinking 125

DMN and Overthinking 126

Stress and Trauma's Impact on Overthinking 128

Mindfulness and Other Interventions 129

Chapter 6: Overcoming Overthinking 133

Strategies 133

Mindfulness and Overthinking 134

CBT and Overthinking 136

Self-Care and Overthinking 139

Action Plan for Overthinking 142

Support from Family and Professionals 144

Chapter 7: Supporting Loved Ones 147

Tips for Supporting Loved Ones with OCD 149

How Can You Support Your Loved Ones? 151

How Can You Take Care of Yourself? 152

Conclusion 155

Bonus Chapter 163

BOOKS BY RICHARD BANKS 192

REFERENCES 194

Introduction

Are you struggling with persistent thoughts and compulsions that are interfering with your daily life? Do you find yourself overthinking and ruminating to the point where it feels like you're stuck in a cycle of worry and anxiety? If so, you are not alone. Millions of people worldwide experience obsessive-compulsive disorder (OCD) and overthinking, which can have a profound impact on their quality of life.

Maybe it was about something terrible that could happen, or perhaps it was something you did that made you feel guilty or ashamed. Maybe it was something you feared would happen—you worried that someone close to you would get sick or die. Or maybe it wasn't even about anything concrete but was just a feeling of dread like something bad was coming.

We all have unique ways of dealing with these thoughts and feelings, but unfortunately, many people who struggle with them suffer in silence. They don't know where to turn for support and guidance on how to deal with their intrusive thoughts.

Intrusive thoughts can be extremely distressing and debilitating—they can make us feel like we're losing control over ourselves. If left untreated, they can lead to clinical conditions such as depression and anxiety disorders.

I have seen firsthand the devastating effects of OCD and overthinking on individuals and their loved ones. These conditions can be overwhelming, isolating, and exhausting, but there is hope. With the right support and treatment, it is possible to manage symptoms and improve your overall well-being.

OCD is a disorder that affects approximately 1% of the

population, and it can be difficult to understand. It is characterized by unwanted thoughts and repetitive behavior—often (but not always) performed to reduce anxiety related to these thoughts.

OCD is defined by the presence of obsessions, compulsions, or both. Obsessions are unwanted and upsetting thoughts, images, or urges that repeatedly enter your mind. Compulsions are behaviors you feel compelled to do in response to an obsession. These can take many forms, from excessively washing or cleaning to checking locks repeatedly or asking for reassurance over and over again.

We all have our routines, and it's important to be able to stick to them. But what happens when your routine gets in the way of your life?

Living with OCD can be a challenge. You might find yourself constantly checking things, or you might find yourself feeling like you have to do things over and over again until they feel just right. It can be hard to manage your time and even harder to explain why you can't make plans with friends or family.

If you think you have OCD, don't worry!

There are ways that you can manage it so that it doesn't take over your life.

If you have OCD, you know it can be challenging. You may feel alone, misunderstood, and isolated from others.

But you're not alone!

OCD can be very debilitating as it can interfere with normal daily activities such as working and going to school. People with OCD find it challenging to control their thoughts and behaviors, despite knowing that they are irrational or excessive. The good news is that effective treatment options are available for those suffering from this condition.

OCD can be especially hard on romantic and platonic relationships because people with OCD often isolate themselves due to shame about their symptoms. In addition, those who are diagnosed with OCD can feel overwhelmed by their symptoms and may find themselves unable to complete daily tasks due to the time they spend managing them.

There are many ways to manage OCD, including medication and therapy. OCD can be debilitating if left untreated, so it's essential to seek treatment as soon as possible if you think you may have symptoms.

It is important to know that there is no one "cure" for OCD. The best way to manage it is by taking steps towards reducing your symptoms and getting more control over your life. Many self-help strategies can help you overcome your symptoms.

It's not just the repetitive thoughts and actions that are challenging—it's also the stigma associated with mental illness. When we hear the word "OCD," we tend to think of people who are very meticulous about their homes or who constantly wash their hands. These things are true for some people with OCD, but they don't represent the whole picture.

People with OCD are often misunderstood

Often, people with OCD feel like they have to do certain

things over and over again because otherwise, they will be "bad" or "unacceptable". They aren't trying to be difficult or weird. They are just struggling with something in their minds that makes it hard for them to relax and enjoy life.

Here are common traits of people living with OCD:

- They don't want to be this way.
- They wish it didn't have to be this way, but they feel like it's not a choice for them.
- They feel like they're not being listened to when people tell them, "There's nothing wrong with you" or "You should just stop".

Dealing with OCD can be daunting, as it can cause your brain to present you with thoughts that don't make sense. However, there are numerous ways to effectively manage this condition. If you suspect that you have OCD, it's essential to reach out and speak with someone about it. Although it may not be easy, seeking support from others can help you understand what's happening in your brain and how to cope with it. This book is also an excellent resource for gaining knowledge about OCD.

Are obsessive thoughts controlling your life?

Are you ready to overcome the struggles of OCD?

Are you ready to find peace of mind and reclaim your life?

If so, then this book is for you. It's a comprehensive guide to understanding, managing, and overcoming obsessive-compulsive disorder (OCD) and intrusive thoughts.

This book provides an in-depth look into the symptoms and diagnostic criteria of OCD, its causes and theories, and the comorbid conditions commonly associated with it. It also includes information on the assessment and diagnosis of OCD, including clinical interviews and laboratory tests. The book further delves into the various treatment options available for OCD, including medications, behavioral and cognitive therapies, psychoanalytic approaches, and combination therapy.

In this book, readers will learn:

1. A deeper understanding of what OCD is and how it affects those with it.

2. Strategies and techniques for managing and coping with the symptoms of OCD, including cognitive-behavioral therapy (CBT) and exposure and response prevention (ERP).

3. Information on accessing professional help and support for OCD, including therapy and medication options.

4. Insight into the latest research on the causes and potential treatments for OCD.

5. Personal stories and perspectives from individuals with OCD that can help to illustrate the challenges and triumphs of living with the condition.

6. Steps to take to improve overall well-being and self-care.

7. Information about how to support loved ones who may have OCD.

This book offers a comprehensive understanding of OCD – from understanding the condition to identifying potential causes and providing effective strategies for treatment. You'll discover that while OCD presents in various forms, the common thread among sufferers is the inability to control their thoughts and behaviors. By delving into the underlying causes of these symptoms, the book provides readers with the tools and knowledge they need to regain control of their lives. Overall, this book is a guide to help individuals overcome and manage OCD and live their best life despite the condition.

Imagine a life where you are no longer held captive by obsessive thoughts and compulsive behaviors. A life where you are in control of your mind, free to live and experience the world to the fullest. This is not just a dream, but a reality you can achieve by reading this book and taking the steps toward managing your OCD. The road to recovery may not be easy, but it is certainly worth it. With the knowledge and tools provided in this book, you can learn to understand and manage your condition and ultimately regain control of your life. So, take a deep breath, and let's begin the journey together. The power to change your life is in your hands, and with this comprehensive guide, you are one step closer to living the life you deserve.

Let's get started!

Chapter 1: The Prevalence and Impact of OCD

What Is OCD?

Obsessive-compulsive disorder (OCD) is a mental health condition characterized by persistent, unwanted thoughts, images, or impulses (obsessions) that lead to repetitive behaviors or mental acts (compulsions). These compulsions are performed in an effort to reduce the anxiety or distress caused by the obsessions. The condition is estimated to affect around 1-2% of the population and can significantly impact a person's quality of life.

Obsessions are defined as recurrent, persistent, and unwanted thoughts, images, or impulses that cause anxiety or distress. These obsessions are often disturbing, and the person may try to ignore or suppress them, but they cannot be eliminated by logic or reasoning. Some common obsessions include fears of contamination, harm, blasphemy, or losing control. Compulsions are defined as repetitive behaviors or mental acts that a person feels driven to perform in response to an obsession or according to rigid rules. These compulsions are typically aimed at preventing or reducing anxiety or distress, or preventing some dreaded event or situation, but they are not connected to the obsession. Some common compulsions include excessive cleaning, counting, checking, praying, or repeating certain words or phrases.

The causes of OCD are not fully understood, but research suggests that a combination of genetic, neurological, and environmental factors may play a role. Studies have shown that OCD is associated with a malfunctioning of the brain's basal ganglia, which is a critical area for controlling movement and behavior. Additionally, an imbalance of certain neurotransmitters, such as serotonin, may be involved.

People with OCD often experience significant impairment in their ability to function in their daily lives. They may have difficulty completing tasks, may avoid certain situations or objects, and may miss school or work. OCD can also lead to feelings of isolation, depression, and anxiety.

HISTORICAL OVERVIEW OF OCD

Obsessive-compulsive disorder (OCD) has been described for centuries under different terms, with some early descriptions dating back to the 16th century. It has variously been conceptualized as a disease of the mind, a form of insanity, a neurosis, and a psychoanalytic construct. Throughout history, the understanding of OCD has evolved, and the current understanding is now based on the latest scientific research.

In ancient Greece and Rome, OCD was known as ***"Morbus sacerdotum"*** (or priest's disease). This term referred to the Catholic priests believed to be affected by this condition and who were likely performing rituals associated with their religious duties while experiencing symptoms of OCD.

In medieval Europe during the Middle Ages, there were many descriptions of people who exhibited repetitive behaviors such as hand washing and praying excessively. Many historians now believe these behaviors may have been early descriptions of OCD symptoms.

The first documented account of OCD was by **Portuguese physician Garcia de Orta in 1563**. He referred to it as *"the disease of cleanliness"* and observed that it was common among people who were "fastidious and neat" in their habits.

The term *"obsessive"* was first used in **1691 by Richard Baxter in his book *The Saint's Everlasting Rest*.** He used it to describe those who are tormented by sinful thoughts and actions. The term *"compulsive"* was coined later by **Dr. William Cullen in 1720** to describe patients who felt compelled to perform certain rituals over and over again.

In the 18th century, **Dr. Samuel Johnson** described the symptoms of OCD as ***"repetitive acts that were senseless but felt necessary."***

In 1844, Dr. Jean-Martin Charcot defined OCD as an illness involving involuntary acts that he believed were driven by repressed sexual urges which could be cured through hypnosis or other means of suggestion therapy (also known as psychoanalysis).

In 1846, psychiatrist Richard Mead proposed that mental illnesses such as anxiety disorders were caused by "over-activity" in the brain.

In 1941, Kurt Schneider developed his classification system for mental illness, which included OCD under his category for obsessive-compulsive personality disorder.

Current Diagnostic Guidelines of OCD

The Diagnostic and Statistical Manual of Mental Disorders (DSM-5) defines obsessive-compulsive disorder as a chronic and debilitating disorder characterized by the presence of recurrent and persistent obsessions or compulsions. It is currently classified as an anxiety disorder in the DSM-5.

According to the DSM-5, OCD symptoms can cause significant distress or impairment in social, occupational, or other areas of functioning. The current diagnostic criteria for OCD include the presence of either obsessions or compulsions, or both, that cause significant distress or impairment in social, occupational, or other areas of functioning.

The symptoms must have been present for at least six months to meet the diagnostic criteria for OCD. In addition, the symptoms cannot be better explained by another psychiatric disorder such as schizophrenia or bipolar disorder.

The DSM-5 lists a few specific symptoms that must be present to diagnose someone with OCD:

1. Recurrent thoughts related to one's own perceived inadequacy or importance
2. Rituals are performed because they provide relief from the resulting anxiety
3. Overvalued ideas about cleanliness
4. Excessive concern with symmetry or exactness

The severity of OCD symptoms can vary significantly from person to person. In general, people with OCD will have at least one obsession or compulsion that they struggle with for at least one hour per day.

OCD PREVALENCE

According to the National Institute of Mental Health, between 1 and 3 percent of people in the United States have OCD. The numbers are even higher in other parts of the world. In Korea, for example, it's estimated that 9% of people suffer from OCD.

The following statistics on the prevalence of OCD have

been provided by the National Institute of Mental Health (NIMH). OCD is estimated to affect 2.2% of adults in the United States, which translates to approximately 1 in 40 individuals. OCD is more common among women than men, with studies showing that women are twice as likely to experience OCD than men. OCD typically begins during childhood or adolescence, with symptoms appearing between the ages of 10 and 13 years old. However, it can also begin in adulthood.

One of the most common misconceptions about OCD is that it's a mental disorder that affects only women. That's not true—OCD can affect anyone, regardless of gender identity. Women are indeed diagnosed with OCD at a rate more than twice as high as men, with almost four times as many women reporting symptoms of the disorder than men. But while the actual disorder is evenly distributed between genders, some cultural factors make OCD more likely to affect women than men.

There are a few reasons that may contribute to this discrepancy.

Women are more likely to seek treatment for mental health issues than men. This is largely due to cultural expectations of "masculinity" and "femininity"—women tend to be perceived as being more emotional and irrational than men, so they're more likely to seek help when they start feeling anxious or depressed.

Men, on the other hand, often feel like they need to be strong and stoic to conform to societal norms about masculinity—so if they're experiencing mental health issues like anxiety or depression, they may not seek help because they don't want others thinking less of them for being vulnerable or "weak".

Why is OCD more common in women?

Studies have shown that women are more likely to be diagnosed with other conditions, such as depression or anxiety, before being diagnosed with OCD. These conditions often co-occur with OCD and can increase the likelihood of developing the disorder.

Additionally, women may be more likely to experience certain types of OCD, such as those related to cleaning, organizing, and perfectionism. These tendencies may be linked to societal expectations and gender roles that place a higher value on cleanliness and organization for women. Furthermore, research suggests that there may be a genetic component to the development of OCD and that hormonal fluctuations during menstrual cycles and pregnancy may also play a role.

Also, women tend to have a higher level of sensitivity than men do, so they're more likely to be bothered by the little things that don't bother others. If you're a woman, this doesn't mean anything bad about you! It just means that it's helpful to know what you're dealing with so that you can take steps toward managing it effectively.

It is important to note that OCD can manifest in various ways and should not be limited to stereotypes. It is important to seek professional help if you suspect that you or a loved one may be experiencing OCD. With the proper treatment, individuals can learn to manage their symptoms and improve their quality of life.

OCD Impact

OCD is a chronic condition that typically develops in adolescence or early adulthood but can also occur in childhood or later in life. The onset of OCD is often gradual, and the symptoms may fluctuate over time.

The impact of OCD on an individual's life can be severe. People with OCD often experience significant impairment in their ability to function in their daily lives. They may have difficulty completing tasks, may avoid certain situations or objects, and may miss school or work. OCD can also lead to feelings of isolation, depression, and anxiety. The condition can also have a significant impact on a person's relationships, as well as their physical and mental health.

Additionally, people with OCD are at a higher risk of developing other mental health conditions such as depression, anxiety, and substance abuse. This can lead to a cycle of poor mental health, which can further exacerbate the symptoms of OCD.

EXPERIENCE INTRUSIVE THOUGHTS

Individuals suffering from OCD may experience intrusive thoughts about things that are not real, such as germs or contamination, leading to compulsive behaviors such as hand washing or cleaning. These behaviors might seem irrational to others, but for someone with OCD, they make sense because they relieve the anxiety caused by these obsessive thoughts.

INTERFERES WITH RELATIONSHIPS

OCD can also interfere with relationships and social interactions—for example, an individual might be unable to keep a job if they are obsessed with certain tasks or rituals at work. Some people with OCD even develop patterns around eating or sleeping that take up a lot of time each day. This can harm their ability to function normally in society because it takes away time that could be spent doing other things like going out with friends or getting an education.

Spend Time and Energy on Unnecessary Thoughts and Behaviors

The most apparent impact of OCD is that it makes individuals who have it spend time and energy on thoughts and behaviors that are not appropriate or rational, which can result in missed opportunities to do more meaningful things. For example, someone with OCD might spend all day thinking about whether they left the stove on when they went to work instead of working on an important project.

Long-term Impact on an Individual's Quality of Life

OCD can have a long-term impact on an individual's quality of life and mental health. In addition to the symptoms themselves, people with OCD often experience depression, anxiety, and stress—all of which can lead to decreased productivity at work or school. People with OCD also often experience problems with maintaining relationships with friends or family members because they may be unable to participate in group activities or social engagements due to their obsessive thoughts and behaviors.

Economic impact

The economic impact of OCD is significant; it affects nearly 2 million Americans each year and costs an estimated $3 billion annually in direct medical costs. Additionally, those with OCD are more likely than others to suffer from other mental illnesses, such as depression or anxiety disorders. The combined cost of these conditions is estimated at $6 billion annually in direct medical costs alone.

Impact on productivity

On a societal level, OCD can greatly impact productivity because it causes people to avoid certain situations or activities and miss out on opportunities for success. In addition, it can be costly for employers who must provide accommodations for employees with OCD-related limitations or problems at work. The condition can lead to decreased productivity and increased absenteeism, which can significantly impact an individual's ability to work and support themselves and their families. Finally, society loses out because of the stigma attached to mental illness, which prevents many people from getting help when they need it most!

Often seen as being "different"

People with OCD are often seen as being "different". They might be ostracized or treated unfairly because they behave differently and may feel isolated. This can harm the person's ability to maintain relationships, as well as their quality of life. The effects of OCD on society are felt through increased stress and anxiety levels in the general population, leading to higher rates of depression and other mental health issues. In addition, numerous costs are associated with treating OCD: mental health professionals, pharmaceuticals, families seeking help for loved ones suffering from the disorder, etc.

Anxiety disorders

People with OCD often have a co-occurring anxiety disorder, such as post-traumatic stress disorder or panic disorder. Anxiety disorders can make it difficult to function normally in everyday life.

DEPRESSION

Depression is common among those who have OCD because they often experience shame and embarrassment related to their condition. They may also feel isolated from others because they don't want anyone else to know about their obsessions or compulsions. Depression makes it harder for people to concentrate on anything other than their symptoms, which furthers the cycle of isolation and shame associated with the disorder.

SLEEP DEPRIVATION

Sleep deprivation is common among those with OCD because they struggle to fall asleep at night due to obsessive thoughts or worries about whether or not they've performed an action correctly (even if it's something simple like locking your front door).

PEOPLE WITH OCD ARE AFRAID

Many people with OCD are afraid or embarrassed to talk about their condition for fear of being judged or having their privacy violated by someone who doesn't understand what they're going through. This leads to a lot of suffering and missed opportunities.

For example, if you have OCD and you're afraid to talk about it because you don't want anyone to know that you have it, then how will you ever find out about support groups or other resources that could help you cope? If you don't know about those resources, what happens when your symptoms get worse? This isn't just an issue for those with OCD—it affects everyone who knows someone with OCD. If we want to make any progress in understanding what causes this illness and how we can help people deal with it successfully, then we need everyone involved in the conversation.

Overthinking, Obsessing, and Overanalyzing

CHAPTER 2: UNDERSTANDING OCD

Obsessive-compulsive disorder (OCD) is a serious mental illness that causes unwanted and repeated thoughts and behaviors. People with OCD experience uncontrollable urges to do things repeatedly or get rid of anxiety-provoking thoughts and images. You may feel like you have to do something, but you don't know why.

OCD worsens when you try to ignore or avoid these thoughts or urges, which causes more stress and anxiety. However, with treatment, you can learn how to stop them before they start—and finally break free from your obsessions.

OCD can make it difficult to function at work, school, or home. It may cause you to miss work or school because of your obsessions or compulsions. It may also cause you trouble sleeping because of the stress caused by your symptoms.

The symptoms of OCD can vary from person to person but typically include the following:

- Obsessions: Recurring and unwanted thoughts, images, or urges that invade your mind; these obsessions often cause severe anxiety or distress
- Compulsions: Repetitive behaviors, such as hand washing, counting, checking things repeatedly, or hoarding items that are not needed or wanted; these repetitive behaviors can be so time-consuming that they interfere with daily life.

Common OCD symptoms include:

- Repetitive behaviors such as hand-washing or checking
- Intrusive thoughts about harm coming to yourself or others (for example, accidentally killing someone)
- Fear of germs and contamination
- Repeatedly thinking about a certain topic (such as bad luck)

Obsessions

Obsessions are repetitive and distressing thoughts, images, or impulses that the person can't control. They're persistent and unwanted, and they repeat in the person's mind over and over again. These thoughts are not just worrying about real-life problems—they're irrational, illogical, and exaggerated. For example, if you have a fear of germs, you might worry that you'll get sick every time you touch something.

People with OCD are convinced that their obsessions are true and must be followed through on to prevent something terrible from happening. This is called "checking" or "contamination obsessions." Other common types of obsessions include:

- Fear of harm coming to self or others
- Need for things to be "just right" or symmetrical
- Fear of making mistakes (such as numbers)
- Fear of saying inappropriate things (such as swearing)
- Excessive religious beliefs

EXAMPLES

Most people have an obsession or two, like the need to make sure all the lights are off before you leave a room or that your house is super-clean. However, if you have OCD, these obsessions can take over your life and make it impossible to do anything else. An obsession is a thought that keeps coming back and won't go away. For example, you might think about whether you locked the door when you left home even though you know for sure that you did it. Or maybe you keep thinking about how dirty the floor is in a room with no dirt.

People with OCD get stuck on these kinds of thoughts

over and over again—they can't stop thinking about them, even though they know logically that what they're thinking isn't true.

Compulsions

Compulsions are actions that you feel compelled to perform over and over again. They usually involve rituals such as washing your hands, touching things in specific ways, avoiding certain places or situations, or counting things over and over again. These compulsions can help temporarily relieve the anxiety caused by obsessions but they also cause more stress because they take up so much of your time—they can take hours each day!

Compulsions are the things you do to make your obsessions disappear. For example, if you're obsessed with germs and think you'll get sick if you don't wash your hands, you might compulsively wash your hands repeatedly. Compulsions can also be behaviors that prevent an obsessive fear from coming true. For example, if you have OCD and think that if you don't check the stove three times before leaving the house, your house will burn down, then checking the stove three times may temporarily relieve this obsession.

Forms of compulsion

Compulsions are behaviors that people with OCD perform to reduce their anxiety. They are often repetitive and can be behaviors that other people would not find strange.

Compulsions can take many forms:

- Repeating an action over and over (e.g., checking the stove)
- Ordering or arranging things a certain way (e.g., lining up all of your pencils)
- Washing your hands repeatedly (e.g., washing your hands for an hour after you touch a doorknob)
- Counting things over and over (e.g., counting every step you take during your walk to work)

Examples

One common compulsion is called "washing" or

"checking." If you have OCD, you may find yourself washing your hands repeatedly or checking that all the doors in your house are locked multiple times before you go to bed.

It's important to remember that these behaviors aren't just about wanting to feel clean or safe; they're also a way for your brain to calm down after experiencing anxiety-inducing thoughts. However, these behaviors aren't helpful in the long run since they don't solve any problems. They tend to make people feel worse about themselves because they're so repetitive and time-consuming!

One of the most common compulsions people with OCD engage in is excessive cleaning. This can range from repeatedly cleaning one's hands or clothing to cleaning and organizing every corner of the house.

Another common compulsion is reassurance seeking. People with OCD will often ask for reassurance that they've done something right or that nothing wrong will happen as a result of what they did. Sometimes this reassurance seeking comes in the form of asking other people to check things over again and again, while other times, it takes the form of checking the same thing repeatedly (for example, constantly checking if the stove is turned off).

OCD sufferers may also engage in excessive washing or grooming behaviors—such as hand washing or showering excessively—and in counting rituals, such as counting steps while walking down stairs or doors while walking through hallways.

Relationship between Obsession and Compulsion

Obsessions are recurring thoughts, images, or impulses that make you feel uncomfortable. They can cause a lot of fear and anxiety, but they're not dangerous. Compulsions are behaviors you do in response to an obsession. For example, if you are obsessed with germs, your compulsion might be hand washing or using antiseptic wipes.

To better manage your OCD symptoms, it's crucial to

understand how obsessions and compulsions work together. Compulsions are the acts people with OCD perform in response to their obsessions. They're often repetitive and may seem odd to others, but they're a way of trying to reduce the anxiety brought on by an obsession.

For example, if someone has an obsessive fear of germs and dirt, they might wash their hands repeatedly to reduce their anxiety when they think about germs. Compulsions can help a person feel better in the moment, but they don't address the root cause of their anxiety or obsessions. OCD is still there.

Compulsions relate to obsessions because they ensure that something negative doesn't happen in the future, even though there's no real reason to think it will. For example, if you are obsessed with getting sick from touching germs, you might wash your hands compulsively so that you don't get sick later on.

For people with OCD, obsessions are like broken records repeatedly playing in their heads. They can be anything—a fear of germs, a worry that they might have hurt someone, or a feeling that they need to do something perfectly.

Some people with OCD also experience what's called "rumination." This is when they think obsessively about something without doing anything at all. It's like playing a broken record on repeat—you're still hearing those same thoughts repeatedly but don't feel like you can do anything about it.

SUBTYPES OF OCD

The subtypes of OCD can be grouped into two categories: obsessions and compulsions. Obsessions are unwanted thoughts, images, or feelings that cause anxiety and distress. Compulsions are repetitive behaviors or mental acts someone feels compelled to do in response to an obsessive thought or image. There are many different types of OCD, and some people may experience more than one type at a time.

These subtypes include:

Hoarding

Hoarding is characterized by the compulsive collection of items with no particular value or use. People who hoard often have trouble discarding things because they feel like they "might need them later." Hoarding is also associated with difficulty organizing items in one's home, leading to clutter and making it difficult to navigate through the space.

Checking

Checking compulsions are those in which people repeatedly check whether or not doors are locked or if they've turned off the stove. Checking rituals can also be used to alleviate anxiety about other things—for example, someone may check his phone at least ten times before going to bed each night because he's worried he'll miss an important text message from his boss.

Pure obsessional OCD

The most common subtype of OCD is called Pure-O (Purely Obsessional). This means the person has obsessions without compulsions associated with them—they just repeatedly have unwanted thoughts. This type of OCD involves persistent thoughts that are distressing but don't necessarily lead to specific actions. For example, you might think that your house is dirty and feel the need to check it repeatedly to make sure it's clean—even though this doesn't make sense because you know your house is clean. You don't actively check it but you do think about it a lot. This is the most common type of OCD and involves obsessions unrelated to a particular theme or topic.

SCRUPULOSITY

Scrupulosity is when someone believes they've committed a sin or broken religious rules by having certain urges or thoughts (like wanting to masturbate). Scrupulosity is typically found in people who practice religion regularly but may not have been raised in one particular faith tradition (such as Taoism). It can also be found in people whose childhoods were filled with rigid religious practices such as prayer rituals or specific dietary restrictions.

Contamination OCD

Contamination OCD involves persistent thoughts and fears about contamination or being dirty. This type of OCD often leads people to develop habits like excessive hand washing, avoiding certain foods or situations (such as public restrooms), and cleaning compulsions like hoarding soiled items or cleaning without being able to stop.

People with contamination obsessions are often very anxious when they come into contact with things they perceive as dirty or unsafe, even if they don't actually make them feel physically dirty or unsafe themselves (for example, when they touch something that has been handled by someone else).

Excessive Doubt

The individual experiences recurrent and persistent thoughts about the possibility that they or others will act in ways that go against their morals and values. They often feel compelled to repeatedly check things such as locks or appliances to ensure they are working properly.

Perfectionism

The individual experiences recurrent and persistent thoughts about being unable to complete tasks perfectly, being unable to meet high expectations set by others, or performing tasks that might result in negative consequences if not performed perfectly. This may lead them to engage in excessive checking behaviors related to the task at hand (e.g., checking homework assignments until they are perfect).

Body dysmorphic disorder

This is when someone becomes obsessed with a perceived defect in their appearance (for example, thinking they're too fat). Body dysmorphic disorder often leads to depression and social isolation because the person avoids going out in public due to appearance concerns.

Some Common Conditions Mistaken for OCD

In treating OCD, it's essential to differentiate it from

other conditions. Here are some common conditions that can be mistaken for OCD:

- Generalized anxiety disorder (GAD)
- Social phobia
- Obsessive-compulsive personality disorder (OCPD)

OCD is a mental health condition with a wide range of symptoms. Many people with OCD also have co-occurring conditions, such as depression or anxiety disorders. It is crucial to treat these conditions together because they can make each other worse. People with OCD are often misdiagnosed initially because their symptoms may seem like another disorder. The following is a list of common conditions that are often mistaken for OCD:

Depression

Depression can cause symptoms similar to OCD, such as anxiety, guilt, and low self-esteem. However, depression usually lasts longer than six months and interferes with your ability to function normally.

Trauma

Trauma can cause symptoms similar to OCD, such as obsessive thoughts about the event and fears related to it. Trauma can also make you feel disconnected from others involved in the traumatic event but not yourself—a symptom called dissociation.

Anxiety disorders

Anxiety disorders may cause obsessions or compulsions similar to those in patients with OCD. You may also experience panic attacks if you have an anxiety disorder.

Personality disorders

Personality disorders are characterized by patterns of thoughts and behaviors that cause distress and affect how we relate to others. They include extreme anxiety, fear, anger, depression, and a distorted way of thinking about ourselves and others. Some people with personality disorders may also experience obsessions and compulsions more regularly than others.

Panic Disorder

Panic disorder is an anxiety disorder that causes feelings of terror, fear, or impending doom without an identifiable trigger or reason. Panic attacks can be so severe that they cause physical symptoms such as chest pain, heart palpitations, and shortness of breath.

Post-Traumatic Stress Disorder (PTSD)

PTSD is an anxiety disorder that develops after experiencing or witnessing a traumatic event such as combat, sexual assault, or natural disaster. People with PTSD often have flashbacks to the event(s) they witnessed or took part in, which is often confused with OCD. It is estimated that nearly 7% of Americans will develop PTSD at some point in their lives.

Eating Disorder

Eating disorders are conditions in which people develop a distorted body image and eating habits. Eating disorders include anorexia nervosa, bulimia nervosa, and binge eating disorder. Anorexia nervosa is characterized by an intense fear of gaining weight and a distorted view of one's own body.

People with anorexia often have severe weight loss, low body weight, and an intense fear of gaining weight. They may also engage in extreme behaviors to maintain their low weight, such as fasting or excessively exercising (sometimes called "exercise bulimia"). People with anorexia may also feel depressed or anxious, have problems concentrating or making decisions, become socially isolated from friends and family members, or abuse drugs or alcohol.

Bulimia nervosa involves episodes of binge eating followed by purging through vomiting or the use of diuretics (medications that cause the kidneys to remove extra water from the body). Bulimics may use other purging methods like laxatives, enemas, and diet pills to prevent weight gain after binge eating.

Binge eating disorder occurs when someone eats large amounts of food within a short period and feels a lack of control over their eating during these episodes.

Substance use disorder

Substance use disorders are associated with obsessive-compulsive disorder (OCD). People who suffer from a substance use disorder tend to experience obsessions and compulsions related to their substance use. For example, a person addicted to alcohol may have an obsession with drinking and a compulsion to drink alcohol. In addition, people with untreated OCD are more likely to develop substance use disorders.

Theories of Causes of OCD

Biological or genetic theory

These theories suggest that OCD is a disorder with genetic components or caused by a chemical imbalance in the brain. Genes can be passed down from parents to their children, which may make a child more likely to develop OCD.

Genetic theories suggest that people with OCD inherit an increased risk of developing the disorder from their parents. These theories hypothesize that genes are associated with susceptibility to developing OCD, but they do not provide specific information about what those genes might be or how they work. It is important to note that many researchers believe environmental factors play a larger role than genetics in influencing whether someone develops OCD.

Neurobiology refers to how brain cells are connected and communicate with one another, which can also be passed down through genetics. These biological factors can play a role in how we think and act, but they do not explain why some people develop OCD while others don't.

Psychological theories

Psychological theories include cognitive and behavioral theories of OCD. The cognitive theory is one of the most widely accepted psychological theories for OCD. This theory suggests that people with OCD have an imbalance in their brain, which causes them to perceive threats where none exist and therefore feel compelled to do things repeatedly to neutralize the perceived threat.

Cognitive theories of OCD focus on how individuals with OCD develop dysfunctional beliefs about their behavior and their world. For example, people with OCD may believe that others will punish them if they do not perform certain actions a certain number of times. They may also believe that bad things will happen if they do not perform these actions (e.g., "I will die if I do not wash my hands").

Cognitive theorists propose that these beliefs lead to distress and anxiety when they are not fulfilled. In turn, this leads to more compulsive behaviors (e.g., hand washing) until the individual feels calm again or until another belief comes into play (i.e., "I must wash my hands because they have germs on them").

Behavioral theory is another psychological theory that suggests that people with OCD have learned behaviors from their environment, especially during childhood. They then continue these behaviors as adults because they have been reinforced by rewards such as praise or avoidance of punishment.

Behavioral theories focus on how the environment

rewards certain behaviors. For example, a person might be rewarded for being clean by getting praise from others and being allowed to play with other clean children. As a result, he will continue to clean himself repeatedly until it becomes an obsession, and he feels like he has no choice but to clean himself more than necessary.

Environmental theories

Environmental theories about the cause of OCD suggest that the disorder is caused by external events in a person's life. For example, traumatic events or stressful situations can trigger OCD symptoms in people who are already prone to it. These triggers might be physical (for example, being injured or exposed to blood) or emotional (for example, feeling guilty). These causes are often related to an individual's genetic makeup or biology.

Another theory is that stress causes OCD. This theory suggests that when we experience stressful events, our bodies release hormones called corticotropin-releasing factor (CRF) and vasopressin, which cause us to feel anxious or depressed. This, in turn, can lead to depression or anxiety disorders like OCD.

Theory of Mind

The Theory of Mind is a theory that suggests that people with OCD have difficulty understanding other people's thoughts and feelings. This theory has been supported by research showing that individuals with OCD often have problems understanding the mental states of others. This may make it difficult for individuals with OCD to interpret their own emotions or those around them accurately, which may result in over-responsibility for actions taken by others or an inability to understand why someone would take certain actions.

Affective Theory

Affective theory suggests that individuals with OCD experience anxiety due to irrational beliefs about themselves and others. For example, an individual might believe that they are responsible for bad things happening to other people or that they are unlovable because they have made mistakes in the past. If this belief is held strongly enough, it could cause significant distress and lead to repetitive behaviors aimed at reducing anxiety related to these beliefs (e.g., checking).

Are You Simply Obsessive or Do You Have Obsessive-compulsive Disorder?

OCD is a mental illness that can make life inconvenient and challenging. It often makes it difficult for people with OCD to maintain relationships, jobs, and personal hygiene. But the good news is that OCD is treatable!

It's important to understand that while the symptoms of OCD may look like healthy habits, they're not. They're repetitive thoughts and behaviors that can cause emotional distress and interfere with your daily life.

How do you know if you have OCD? The first step is to identify if you are simply obsessing or if it has taken over your life and caused real problems in your relationships and work life.

Here's how to tell the difference between normal behavior and obsessive-compulsive behavior.

Example 1

Normal thinking: You buy a new pair of shoes and think about them every day until you can wear them again.

Obsessive thinking: You can't stop thinking about the new pair of shoes, even when they're not on your feet. You keep thinking about what they look like, how they would look to other people, etc. This goes on for longer than just one day (or even one week).

Example 2

Normal thinking: Planning to go to the grocery store to buy ingredients for dinner tonight.

Obsessive thinking: Continuously thinking about the possibility of running out of a specific ingredient while at the grocery store, even though it is well-stocked, and becoming anxious at the thought of not being able to make dinner as planned. This anxiety continues even after returning home with the necessary ingredients.

Example 3

Normal thinking: Checking emails and responding to important ones.

Obsessive thinking: Constantly checking and re-checking emails, even when there is no new message, and becoming anxious if unable to check emails for some time. This can negatively impact the person's productivity and relationships with others.

Example 4

Normal thinking: Planning a vacation and looking forward to it.

Obsessive thinking: Continuously thinking and planning every detail of the vacation, to the point that it causes anxiety and stress, and not being able to enjoy the actual vacation because of this preoccupation.

Here are some additional signs that indicate you may have OCD:

- You feel like your actions are being watched by others (even if they aren't).
- You're afraid of making mistakes.
- You have to check things over and over again until they feel right.
- You have trouble thinking about anything other than the thing that's bothering you.
- If you don't perform certain rituals (like washing your hands), you feel like something bad will happen.
- You feel like you need to be perfect at everything to be happy or successful.

Overthinking, Obsessing, and Overanalyzing

Chapter 3: Coping with OCD

If you or someone you know has obsessive-compulsive disorder, you probably know that this condition has real, tangible effects on your daily life and relationships.

The Impact of OCD on Daily Life

When you have OCD, your life can feel very different from the lives of other people.

You might find yourself constantly doubting your thoughts and actions or feeling like you can't make decisions because you're afraid that something bad will happen if you do. When you have OCD, it's hard to know whether the things happening in your head are real, which is why it can be so hard to tell if your fears are justified.

OCD AND RELATIONSHIPS

Regarding relationships, OCD can also impact how you relate to others—and what kind of relationships you can create. Some people with OCD feel awkward around others because they fear being judged for their behavior or rituals. Others feel like they need to keep their symptoms hidden from others so that no one knows about them—and this can lead to feelings of isolation over time.

Often, these feelings cause people with OCD to withdraw from social situations or avoid certain situations altogether—even when they would otherwise enjoy these activities! However, even though it may seem impossible at times, there are ways to cope with these issues and live a more fulfilling life despite having OCD.

Being vulnerable is hard when we're focused on our

anxieties and fears. It can also affect how well you communicate with the people closest to you. If we don't tell our partners how we're feeling or what's going on with us, they may feel like they're being left out of the loop or that something is wrong with them because they aren't getting enough attention from us (not true!). We need our partners' support during these difficult times.

THE IMPACT OF OCD ON WORK LIFE AND SCHOOL

OCD can take a toll on all areas of your life: your job, personal relationships, and even your health. For example, it may impact your ability to perform well at work or school. You might feel like you're letting people down when you can't keep up with all the things that need to be done- and that's not fair to them or yourself!

Your symptoms can greatly impact your work and school life. You may have trouble concentrating in class or working at a job that does not involve your passion.

You may struggle with organization and time management at work because you spend too much time trying to get things done perfectly, causing you to miss deadlines or not finish projects on time. You might also have trouble delegating tasks to coworkers because you want them done "right," and you don't trust others enough to allow them to do it their way.

In school, the same thing can happen—you might spend too much time trying to get things right instead of just doing them well enough to be acceptable by others' standards. Because of this tendency, you might have trouble passing exams or completing assignments on time due to procrastination caused by perfectionism (e.g., spending hours rereading books instead of just reading them once through quickly).

Let's look at some of the ways that OCD can impact your work life:

-If you're an entrepreneur, OCD can make you hyper-focused on details and processes, which could help you streamline your business and make it run more smoothly. The downside is that it may also prevent you from taking risks or making quick decisions when necessary.

-If you're a salaried employee, OCD might make you feel like you need to complete every task perfectly for it to be considered complete. This could stifle your creativity and cause problems if the company needs someone who can think outside of the box.

-If your job involves working with people face-to-face (like sales or customer service), then having OCD could lead to social anxiety, awkwardness, and difficulty communicating clearly because of the constant worry about what other people think of you (and your performance).

STRATEGIES FOR MANAGING SYMPTOMS

It can be challenging to manage your symptoms and improve your quality of life. Some strategies can help you get started, though.

First, let's talk about what makes OCD so challenging. For one thing, it's invisible—you can't see or feel it, which means you don't always know when it's there. For another thing, OCD is kind of sneaky: it tends to pop up when we're busy or stressed out (and then make us even more busy and stressed because we're trying to deal with it). And finally, OCD is just... weird! It makes our brains do things that might seem strange to other people.

So what can we do?

Well, first off: know yourself.

What are the symptoms of your OCD?

Where do they usually show up?

Write them down or make a list to have them handy when you need them later.

Here are some strategies for managing your symptoms and improving your quality of life:

TALK TO A PROFESSIONAL

OCD is a serious disorder, but there are ways to manage it. If you're feeling overwhelmed by OCD and want to learn more about treatment options, reach out to a therapist or other mental health professional in your area today!

PRACTICE RELAXATION TECHNIQUES

Relaxation is an integral part of managing OCD because when we're stressed out and anxious, it's hard to think clearly and make good decisions. Try meditating regularly or taking some time every day to just sit quietly with no distractions around you—this will help clear your mind so that you can focus on relaxing instead of ruminating over what might happen if something bad happens. You could also try yoga or another form of exercise that helps calm both body and mind down—whatever works for you!

AVOID CERTAIN SITUATIONS

Try to avoid situations that trigger your obsessions. If you know you're going to be around something that makes you anxious, try to avoid it or be prepared ahead of time for what might happen.

USE DISTRACTIONS

Distract yourself with a positive thought or activity whenever possible. This can help break up the cycle of OCD thoughts and give you some relief from them.

PROPER SLEEP

Try to get enough sleep and exercise regularly, as they contribute to good health and reduce stress levels, which can help improve OCD symptoms. It's hard to feel good when you're tired, so try getting 7-9 hours of sleep each night. You can also try taking naps during the day if you're having trouble sleeping at night—just be sure not to take too many naps, or they'll interfere with your nighttime sleep cycle!

EAT NUTRITIOUS FOOD

Eating healthily helps keep your body strong and healthy, reducing stress levels! Make sure you're eating plenty of fruits and vegetables daily—they're packed with vitamins, fiber, and nutrients that give you energy without gaining weight!

Get organized!

One way to do this is by making a list of things that need to be done and crossing them off as you go—that way, you'll always know what needs to happen next and where your time goes!

Use positive affirmations

Do this when you're feeling down about yourself or your situation. For example, "I am strong" or "I am capable". They don't have to be true at the moment—they just need to state your goals and make you feel better!

Make a list

Make lists of things that make you happy or things that make other people happy—anything from a favorite food to a good memory from childhood—and keep them somewhere easy for yourself or others to see when you're feeling down or anxious about something happening in the future.

Change your perspective

Try changing your perspective on OCD. Instead of thinking about it as something that "has" you, think about it as something you have control over. The more control you have, the less power OCD has over you.

Self-help Techniques and Coping Skills

Here are some tips you can do to help yourself when you feel like you're having an OCD episode.

- First, be aware of your symptoms and how they might affect your life. If you notice that something is getting in the way of your normal activities or causing problems for you, it may be worth looking into.
- Second, remember that everyone has a bad day sometimes. Don't let these moments define who you are as a person or make you feel ashamed or embarrassed—they are just part of life!

- Third, try not to overthink things too much. If something goes wrong and makes you feel anxious or upset, don't panic! Just remind yourself that this is normal and happens to everyone sometimes (even if it doesn't seem like it).
- Fourth, take deep breaths until the feeling passes. You can even set the alarm on your phone or computer so that no one around you knows what's happening inside your head!

Mindfulness-based Interventions and Stress Management Techniques

Mindfulness-based interventions and stress management are two types of therapy that can help you manage your obsessive-compulsive disorder (OCD).

Mindfulness

Mindfulness is a technique that can be used to manage

stress, but it's also a way of approaching the world. It helps us catch ourselves when we're thinking negatively, such as with obsessive thoughts about something that happened in the past or anxiety about something that might happen in the future. When we're mindful, we're focused on being aware of what's happening in the present moment instead of worrying about the past or future.

When we're stressed out and anxious, our minds tend to go into overdrive and start spinning out of control with all kinds of negative thoughts. Mindfulness practice can help us bring our minds back down to earth by reminding us that these thoughts are just that: thoughts. They don't need to be acted upon immediately or given more weight than they deserve.

When you feel overwhelmed by an obsessive thought, try this exercise: sit down somewhere quiet where you won't be interrupted (or take a walk), close your eyes, and focus on your breathing for 30 seconds or so. Then open your eyes and look around at what's happening right now—what do you see? What sounds are there? What smells can you identify? How does your body feel right now? Stay focused.

Mindfulness practice involves paying attention to the present moment with an attitude of openness and acceptance. There are different types of meditation, but many people start by focusing on their breath. When you're practicing mindfulness, you'll notice any thoughts that pop into your head, but you won't judge them as good or bad—you'll let them pass through your mind like clouds passing across the sky.

It can help people with OCD by allowing them to step back from their obsessive thoughts, which allows them to see the irrationality of their obsessions and compulsions. Mindfulness can also help people learn how to tolerate distress without engaging in compulsive behavior.

STRESS MANAGEMENT

Stress management can also help reduce the intensity of symptoms by helping you cope better with difficult situations. Stress management includes deep breathing, meditation, yoga, and other relaxation exercises that can lower your heart rate and blood pressure and increase feelings of calmness and peace.

ORGANIZATIONAL AND TIME-MANAGEMENT STRATEGIES

While it's true that OCD is a mental disorder, it can also be treated like any other medical condition. One of the best ways to treat OCD is with organizational and time-management strategies. The first step in this process is determining how your OCD affects your life.

Do you have trouble keeping organized?

Are you constantly running late?

Do you forget important appointments?

These are all symptoms of a larger problem – the inability to manage your time effectively. If this sounds like something that has been affecting your life for years, then it might be time to seek professional help.

TIPS TO KEEP YOURSELF ORGANIZED

Need some help getting organized? Here are a few tips.

1. Try to keep your desk clean and clear of clutter. If you have too many papers and notebooks on top, it will make it hard for you to find what you need when you need it.
2. Make sure that all of your papers have a place where they go every time you take them out of a folder or binder. For example, if you receive a lot of mail, save bills in one envelope and return letters to the sender in another envelope. This way, when the mail comes in, all of the bills will go in one box while the letters go into another box!
3. Make sure that all of your files are organized by date so that if someone asks for an old document or report, it will be easy for them to find what they need without having to look through all of the other documents and reports in each file folder/binder (or drawer).

Tips for Managing Your Tasks or Time

1. Set a schedule and stick to it.
2. Do the most important tasks first.
3. Prioritize tasks in order of importance, then by the deadline.
4. Break down large tasks into smaller ones that can be completed within your time frame.
5. Keep a list of daily, weekly, monthly, and yearly goals.
6. Use an electronic calendar to keep track of appointments and deadlines.
7. Keep a planner or notebook with you at all times and write down things you need to remember while they're fresh in your mind.
8. Use an app like Google Calendar or Outlook to organize your life.
9. Try setting reminders on your phone for important events or tasks.

Support Resources

If you or someone you love has OCD, there are many ways to get help.

SUPPORT GROUPS

Support groups can be a great place to meet others who understand what you're going through and to share experiences. You can also find out about local treatment options and other available resources.

ONLINE RESOURCES

There are many online resources available to help people with OCD. Many of these sites offer information on treatment options, tips for managing symptoms at home, and more.

PROFESSIONALS

If you have OCD or someone you love has OCD, you know how difficult it can be to find the right help. Various professionals specialize in treating OCD and anxiety disorders but they all have different approaches, and some work better than others. The key is to find the type of professional that speaks to you and makes you feel like they understand what you're going through.

Many types of experts can help people with OCD and anxiety disorders: psychologists, psychiatrists, social workers, counselors, therapists, and more. Each one will have a different specialty and approach when dealing with these issues. You want to find someone who fits into your life as much as possible—and that means finding someone with experience working with people suffering from OCD-related problems.

To find the right person for your needs:

- Make sure that the person has experience in treating OCD patients.

- Ask about their approach (i.e., cognitive-behavioral therapy).

FINDING THE RIGHT PROFESSIONAL HELP

It can be hard to know where to start when you're looking for help with OCD.

When finding the right professional help, the first thing to do is talk with your doctor. He or she may be able to point out several options in your area, including support groups and other resources.

Your doctor may also be able to recommend a therapist or psychiatrist who specializes in treating OCD. If your doctor isn't familiar with treating OCD and has no suggestions for professionals in your area, ask if someone else at their practice could help.

You may also want to consider asking friends or family members for recommendations. They may know someone who has experience treating OCD or who has helped them through similar situations in the past.

Medications Used to Treat OCD

The medications used to treat obsessive-compulsive disorder (OCD) include selective serotonin reuptake inhibitors (SSRIs) and others.

Selective serotonin reuptake inhibitors (SSRIs)

Serotonin is a chemical that helps regulate mood and sleep. Selective serotonin reuptake inhibitors (SSRIs) are a class of medications used to treat obsessive-compulsive disorder (OCD). These drugs work by increasing the amount of serotonin in your brain. If you have too little serotonin, you may experience depression or difficulty sleeping.

Other medications used to treat OCD include:

- Antidepressants called tricyclics, which act on other neurotransmitters in your brain (such as norepinephrine)
- Antipsychotics are used primarily to treat symptoms such as delusions and hallucinations.

BEHAVIORAL AND COGNITIVE THERAPIES

If you have OCD, there's no need to suffer in silence. Behavioral and cognitive therapies can be very effective at treating the symptoms of this mental illness.

Behavioral therapy for OCD consists of a series of steps that help you learn how to manage the disorder and cope with your symptoms. It's important to understand that behavioral therapy is not a cure—it's a way of managing your symptoms so they don't interfere with your life as much.

Cognitive therapy

Cognitive therapy also helps people with OCD learn new ways of thinking about their condition. It can help them change their perception of reality and see things more positively, decreasing their stress levels and allowing them to function better overall.

This therapy is designed to help you change how you think about your obsessions and compulsions. It also teaches you how not to get so caught up in your thoughts and feelings, which will help reduce your anxiety levels.

Exposure and response prevention (ERP)

Exposure and response prevention (ERP) is a cognitive behavioral therapy that helps people with obsessive-compulsive disorder (OCD) manage their symptoms by exposing them to what they fear but preventing them from engaging in compulsive behaviors.

ERP involves exposing yourself to the things that trigger your obsessions but not allowing yourself to perform any associated rituals. For example, if you fear germs, you might be exposed to things containing germs (such as a public toilet). This type of therapy is often used in conjunction with cognitive therapy. The goal is to learn that nothing bad will happen if you don't perform rituals or compulsions.

The idea behind ERP is that when we are faced with something we fear, our brains often try to protect us from feeling uncomfortable by telling us that we need to do something about it—even when that something makes no sense or isn't helpful at all.

Mindfulness meditation

This involves sitting quietly and focusing on breathing deeply and slowly while also noticing other sights and sounds around you without judging them as good or bad. This helps reduce anxiety levels.

The Role of Psychoanalytic Approaches in the Treatment of OCD

Psychoanalytic treatments for OCD are based on the idea that unconscious conflicts and irrational thoughts cause the disorder. According to this theory, people with OCD develop their symptoms as a way to try to resolve these conflicts.

The psychoanalytic approach to OCD is based on the idea that compulsions are unconscious attempts at relieving anxiety caused by a conflict between the ego and superego or between the id and superego. To understand the role of psychoanalytic approaches in treating OCD, it is important to understand how this approach views compulsions.

Compulsions are seen as unconscious attempts at relieving anxiety caused by a conflict between the ego and superego or between the id and superego. This conflict may be due to an imbalance in any of these areas (id, ego, and superego) or because they operate differently than they should. The psychoanalytic approach assumes that these conflicts can be resolved through interpretation by a therapist trained in this approach.

This treatment focuses on helping patients become aware of their unconscious processes and working through them. For example, if patients fear germs and clean constantly, they may unconsciously try to avoid feeling dirty or unworthy. A psychoanalytic therapist might help the patient understand these associations and find ways to challenge them rather than just telling them not to clean so much.

PSYCHOANALYSIS AND ITS CRITICISMS

Psychoanalysis is a psychodynamic approach that focuses on the relationship between conscious and unconscious thoughts. The goal of psychoanalysis is to help people understand their unconscious thoughts, feelings, and motivations so they can change their behavior. Psychoanalysis is used to treat a variety of mental health problems, including obsessive-compulsive disorder (OCD).

Psychoanalysis has been criticized for being too time-consuming and expensive, as well as not always being effective. Some criticize it for its focus on early childhood experiences. However, some people with OCD who have tried other treatments have found that psychoanalysis helps them manage their symptoms better than other approaches.

Psychoanalysis can be done through individual psychotherapy or group therapy sessions. The goals of psychoanalytic therapy for OCD include helping patients understand how their symptoms relate to their past experiences, learning how to cope with stress and negative emotions, and improving social skills and communication skills so that they can interact more effectively with others without having unwanted thoughts or behaviors pop up in response; this may also involve working through any problems related to the patient's family life growing up.

Psychoanalysis is based on three major principles:

1. The unconscious mind is where our repressed thoughts and feelings are stored; they influence our

behaviors without our awareness of them.

2. Trauma can cause repression and lead to neurosis (a type of mental disorder).

3. Free association (the patient's ability to say whatever comes to mind) is a key part of understanding the unconscious mind, dreams, and other causes of neurosis.

Object Relations Theory and Its Criticisms

Object Relations Theory is one of the most common psychoanalytic approaches to the treatment of OCD. It focuses on the relationship between an individual and their environment—or, more specifically, on how that individual's relationship with objects in their environment affects their behavior. One of the main criticisms of the theory is that it fails to address causality – while it may be true that an individual's relationship with objects in their environment can affect their behavior, how do we know which came first? Did the object cause the behavior, or was it a result of some other factor?

Object Relations Theory is based on the idea that all individuals have three parts – the id, ego, and superego. The id is driven by biological needs, while the superego regulates those desires by imposing moral rules upon them. The ego serves as the mediator between these two forces by weighing the pros and cons of each action before deciding what behavior is appropriate in any given situation. Those suffering from OCD have false egos that do not make rational decisions about right vs. wrong actions, causing them to repeatedly engage in repetitive rituals such as washing hands until they feel clean enough to stop repeating this behavior.

Object Relations Theory has been criticized for its lack of empirical evidence supporting its claims about how psychodynamic therapy can be used successfully to treat people who suffer from OCD.

One criticism of this approach is that it ignores biological factors such as genetics or brain chemistry in explaining why someone develops OCD. Another criticism is that it does not consider how much of what we learn about other people comes from direct experience rather than from internalizing ideas from others' behavior.

COMBINATION THERAPY AND TREATMENT RESISTANCE

Combination therapy is a treatment method that combines two or more therapies to treat a mental health disorder. Combination therapy is commonly used to treat obsessive-compulsive disorder (OCD).

The combination of behavioral therapy with medication is more effective than either method alone. However, some people respond better to one type of treatment or another, so your doctor may recommend trying different combinations of therapies before deciding which works best for you.

Treatment resistance occurs when a patient does not respond well to treatment. It can be frustrating for the patient and their doctor, but it's important not to give up! Your doctors will likely change your treatment plan as needed until they find something that works for you. If all else fails, there are other options available that may be able to help.

You should always consult a doctor for any medications or treatments you plan to use for OCD. Many people with OCD resist treatment and will need combination therapy to get the best results. For example, you might need medication and cognitive behavioral therapy (CBT) to help you manage your symptoms.

How to manage treatment-resistant OCD

If you're suffering from treatment-resistant OCD, there are still ways to manage the symptoms. If you've tried multiple medications or psychotherapies and are still experiencing symptoms, it's important to look at what might contribute to the problem.

One thing to consider is that OCD can be a secondary diagnosis for other conditions, like bipolar disorder or depression. These conditions can have their own symptoms that could make it difficult for your doctor to diagnose and treat your OCD successfully.

Another thing to consider is that there may be an environmental trigger for your symptoms that isn't being addressed by therapy or medication. This means that even if you find something that works for a while if the trigger isn't eliminated, you'll eventually start experiencing symptoms again.

To manage treatment resistance effectively, it's important to work with a team of professionals who can help you identify what's causing your symptoms and address them accordingly, so they don't come back once they've gone away.

FUTURE RESEARCH IN OCD

In the past few decades, researchers have made significant advances in understanding obsessive-compulsive disorder. These advances have been helped by new techniques such as functional Magnetic Resonance Imaging (fMRI), which allow researchers to look at brain activity in real time.

Many areas of research continue to be explored for OCD. One area is the relationship between genes and OCD. Scientists know that there is a genetic component to the development of some forms of OCD. However, they do not yet understand how this happens or relates to other factors contributing to developing OCD.

Another area of research involves understanding what causes obsessive thoughts and compulsive behaviors. Scientists are trying to understand if these differences are based on differences in brain structure, function, or perhaps even something else entirely! Some people with OCD feel that their thoughts are completely out of control, while others believe they can control them if they try hard enough.

Another area that deserves more attention is treatment options for children with OCD. Currently, there is no medication approved.

Advance in Neuroimaging

Advances in neuroimaging and other laboratory studies have provided critical information about the neurobiological mechanisms of OCD. However, these advances have also highlighted some important gaps in our understanding of this disorder. For instance, neuroimaging studies show that brain regions involved in obsessive-compulsive symptoms are activated during symptom provocation; however, it is unclear whether these same regions are activated during functional impairment and when patients are not experiencing their symptoms.

Advances in neuroimaging and other laboratory studies have provided valuable information about the brain's response to OCD symptoms, but much of this research is still in its early stages. As such, it is difficult to determine exactly how the findings will be used to inform the treatment of OCD in the future.

Need for new pharmacological and psychological plans

While there have been advances in treating OCD, it is still one of the most challenging mental disorders to treat. This is especially true for individuals with severe symptoms and high levels of impairment. There is much room for future research on OCD.

There are many areas where further research could be done to improve our understanding of the disorder and how best to treat it. For example, we need more studies that compare different types of therapy (such as cognitive-behavioral therapy and exposure response prevention) directly against one another to determine which is most effective for different patient populations or subtypes of OCD (e.g., specific phobias).

In addition, there is a need for more studies that compare pharmacological treatments with each other (e.g., venlafaxine versus clomipramine). Finally, there is a need for more studies that assess how patients respond when they stop taking their medications after having been on them for an extended period (e.g., 6 months) so that we can better assess whether medication should be continued indefinitely or not.

IMPORTANCE OF RESEARCH ON OCD

Research on OCD has made incredible strides in recent years, but there's still a lot to learn about this complex disorder. The impact of OCD on people's lives can be enormous. It can cause significant distress and impairment, affecting their work, social life, and quality of life.

New research on OCD will help us better understand the causes of this condition so we can develop more effective treatments, improve our understanding of what works best for different types of patients, and ultimately improve the quality of life for those suffering.

Chapter 4: Overthinking and OCD

Overthinking is a common symptom of Obsessive-Compulsive Disorder (OCD), characterized by repetitive thoughts and behaviors that intrude on the person's daily life. The thoughts and behaviors can become so overwhelming that they interfere with daily functioning or cause significant distress in the person's life.

Different types of overthinking include rumination, worry, and catastrophizing.

RUMINATION

Rumination is when you constantly go over the same thoughts or situations in your head, often negative ones. This is when you repetitively focus on negative thoughts. You go over the same negative thoughts repeatedly, often in an attempt to find a solution or answer. This can lead to depression, anxiety, as well as other symptoms of OCD. Rumination is different from worry because your focus is on the thought itself. Worry is more about future events and what may or may not happen.

WORRY

Worry is when you have negative expectations about things that may happen in the future—for example, thinking that something bad will happen because you forgot to lock your door. This is similar to rumination, but it's usually focused more on future events than present ones.

Worrying about the future involves going over what could happen if certain things were to occur, which can lead to anxiety and depression if it persists for long periods. As with rumination, this can lead to depression, anxiety, and other symptoms of OCD.

Catastrophizing

Catastrophizing involves believing something bad will happen instead of worrying about it; this type of thinking is also known as "all-or-nothing thinking." Catastrophic thinkers believe that if something bad happens (or even if they just imagine something bad happening), they won't be able to handle it—so they may avoid certain situations altogether, so they don't have to face their fears or challenges.

Catastrophizing is when you think the worst possible outcome will happen in any situation—for example, thinking that if you don't get an A on this test, then you won't pass your class and won't graduate high school at all! Like rumination and worry, catastrophizing can also lead to depression, anxiety, and other symptoms of OCD.

INTRUSIVE THOUGHTS

Intrusive thoughts are unwanted, frequent thoughts, images, or urges that cause anxiety, distress, or difficulty functioning. They are usually experienced as coming from outside of the person rather than from their own mind.

Intrusive thoughts can take many forms, including:

- Fear of being contaminated by germs (e.g., by shaking hands with someone)
- Fear of harming others (e.g., by having a violent thought about someone)
- Fear of acting on impulse (e.g., by having a sexual thought about someone you know)
- Fear of thinking blasphemous thoughts (e.g., imagining a religious figure naked)

INTRUSIVE THOUGHTS VS. OCD THOUGHTS

Intrusive thoughts are a type of thought that is not

under conscious control. The person may not be aware that they have them, but they still have the same effect on their behavior. For example, you may notice yourself thinking about something and perhaps even acting on it. However, you may not be aware of this thought or why you have it.

In obsessive-compulsive disorder (OCD), people experience frequent and unwanted thoughts resulting in intrusive behaviors or mental rituals. These rituals can be simple (such as checking locks more often than necessary) or complex (such as washing hands repeatedly).

If you suffer from OCD, your thoughts are triggered by certain situations or events, such as anxiety or stress, being around someone with dirt on their hands, or touching something considered dirty.

What Are the Different Factors That May Contribute to Overthinking?

Biological factors

Biological factors such as genes and brain chemistry may influence your tendency to overthink. If you have a family history of OCD or another anxiety disorder, such as generalized anxiety disorder (GAD), you are more likely to develop OCD yourself. This is because certain genes have been shown to increase your risk of developing these conditions.

Psychological factors

Many psychological factors contribute to the development of intrusive thoughts.

One of these is past experiences. If you've been through something traumatic in the past, your thoughts might be more likely to turn negative. For example, if you were abused as a child or exposed to violence regularly, your thoughts may be more likely to focus on those situations.

Another factor is mental health. If you have a mental illness like depression or anxiety, then it's likely that your intrusive thoughts will be more intense than normal. Depression and anxiety can cause people to ruminate over negative events from their pasts or imagine future scenarios that put them in danger (or both). Those who suffer from these conditions might also experience an increase in their overall level of anxiety about everyday life events—even ones that would normally not trigger such feelings.

External Factors

External factors, including stress and other environmental factors, often trigger intrusive thoughts. Stress is a common trigger for overthinking, as it can cause you to become hyper-aware of your thoughts and actions. When stressed out, your brain will often try to find ways of distracting itself by engaging in obsessive thought patterns.

Other common triggers include boredom and unmet

needs. If you aren't engaged in activities that are meaningful to you—or if you're feeling bored because there's nothing to do—you may begin overthinking to fill the void.

Overthinking can also be triggered by unmet needs. For example, if you're hungry but don't have any food in the house or if there's something else that's missing from your life (like a relationship or a career), then this can lead to an increase in obsessive thinking about what might be going wrong or what could be done differently.

IMPACT OF OVERTHINKING

Overthinking can have negative effects on work, relationships, and overall happiness. In terms of work, overthinking can lead to procrastination, decreased productivity, and difficulty making decisions. In relationships, overthinking can cause communication issues and lead to feelings of insecurity and mistrust. Additionally, overthinking can increase stress and anxiety, negatively impacting overall happiness and well-being.

Overthinking can be a great tool but also a tremendous distraction. It can keep you from making the right decision and from doing what you need to do to succeed.

Here are some of the biggest effects of overthinking on your work, relationships, and overall happiness.

AT WORK

When you overthink at work, it is often because you are afraid of making a mistake or letting someone down. This leads to lower productivity because instead of focusing on your job and getting it done, you are wasting time worrying about what could go wrong or how things might turn out if something goes wrong. When this happens regularly, it can lead to burnout, poor performance reviews, and low self-esteem.

IN RELATIONSHIPS

When you overthink in relationships, it will lead to anxiety about whether or not someone likes you back or feels the same way about things as you do. This can cause issues with trust and communication between partners because one might decide not to tell their partner something important because they think it would make them upset or angry instead of just being honest about what's happening in their lives right now (or even yesterday!). This can lead to feelings of loneliness or isolation.

OVERALL HAPPINESS

We've all been there: you're trying to relax or have a nice time with friends and family, but you just can't stop thinking about something. Sure, it could be work—but it could be something way more important. Overthinking can be stressful, and it can also take a toll on your overall happiness. If you're overthinking too much, here's what might happen:

1) You'll feel like you're always worrying about everything.

2) You won't be able to focus on anything else, even if the thing you're worried about isn't that big of a deal.

3) You'll feel stressed out because of all the extra energy required to keep up with your thoughts.

4) You may start panicking about things that aren't actually scary at all!

Negative Effects of Overthinking

Overthinking can have negative effects on both physical and mental health too. Some of the most common negative effects include:

Sleep disturbances

Overthinking can make it difficult to fall asleep at night and lead to insomnia. This can result in feelings of fatigue and grogginess during the day, making it difficult to focus and complete tasks.

Fatigue

Constant overthinking can be mentally and emotionally exhausting, leading to feelings of fatigue throughout the day.

Decreased cognitive function

Overthinking can lead to cognitive overload, making it

difficult to focus and process information. This can result in decreased cognitive function, including poor memory and difficulty with decision-making.

Depression and anxiety

Overthinking can also lead to negative thoughts and emotions, such as depression and anxiety. These mental health conditions can impact overall well-being and quality of life.

Stress

Overthinking can cause stress, leading to physical symptoms such as headaches, muscle tension, and a weakened immune system.

Physical health problems

Overthinking can lead to many physical health problems, including high blood pressure, heart disease, and a weakened immune system.

Substance abuse

Overthinking can cause individuals to turn to drugs or

alcohol as a way to cope with their negative thoughts and emotions.

Isolation

Overthinking can lead to social isolation and fear of social interactions.

It is important to note that overthinking can also be a symptom of other mental health conditions, such as anxiety disorders and depression, and if you are experiencing any of the above effects of overthinking, it is best to speak with a mental health professional.

Overthinking Case Studies

Sarah is a young professional who has always been a high achiever. She is constantly thinking about her work and career and feels a constant sense of pressure to excel. She finds it difficult to relax and unwind and often stays up late at night worrying about her job. As a result, Sarah has developed insomnia and fatigue throughout the day. Her overthinking has also led to anxiety and depression, and she has struggled to find a balance in her life.

John is a college student who is struggling with overthinking. He constantly worries about his grades and future and finds it difficult to focus on his studies. He has developed insomnia, and he feels exhausted throughout the day. He's also developed social anxiety and avoids social interactions. He's also turned to substance abuse to cope with his negative thoughts and emotions.

Jane is a stay-at-home mother who is struggling with overthinking. She constantly worries about her children and their safety and finds it difficult to relax and enjoy her time with them. She has developed insomnia, and she feels fatigued throughout the day. Her overthinking has also led to anxiety and depression, and she has struggled to find a balance in her life.

Mark is a retiree who is struggling with overthinking. He has developed insomnia, and he feels fatigued throughout the day. He constantly worries about his health and finances and finds it difficult to relax and enjoy his retirement. His overthinking has also led to anxiety and depression, and he has struggled to find a balance in his life.

As the above examples show, overthinking can significantly impact an individual's life. It can lead to sleep disturbances, fatigue, decreased cognitive function, depression, anxiety, stress, and even physical health problems. It can also lead to social isolation, substance abuse, and other negative impacts. If you are struggling with overthinking, it is important to seek help from a mental health professional.

THE CONNECTION BETWEEN OVERTHINKING AND OCD

Overthinking is a common symptom of OCD, as obsessions can lead to excessive rumination and worrying. For example, an individual with OCD may be obsessed with cleanliness and spend excessive time thinking about germs and contamination. This can lead to overthinking how to prevent contamination and clean oneself and one's surroundings. Similarly, an individual with OCD may have an obsession with harming someone and spend excessive time thinking about how to prevent it.

Overthinking in OCD is not only limited to obsessions but also compulsions. Individuals with OCD may engage in mental compulsions such as repetitive prayers, counting, or repeating phrases to neutralize the obsessions. These compulsions can lead to overthinking as they are time-consuming and can lead to cognitive overload.

It is also worth noting that while overthinking is a symptom of OCD, it is not limited to individuals with OCD and can be present in other mental health conditions.

Difference between Overthinking and OCD

Overthinking and OCD are related, but they are not the same thing. The main difference between the two is that overthinking is a symptom, while OCD is a mental health disorder.

Obsessions

As we've said, OCD is characterized by persistent, unwanted thoughts, images, or impulses (obsessions) that lead to repetitive behaviors or mental acts (compulsions). Overthinking, on the other hand, refers to excessive and prolonged thinking about something. While overthinking can be a symptom of OCD, it can also occur in individuals without OCD.

Compulsions

Individuals with OCD engage in repetitive behaviors or mental acts (compulsions) to neutralize or counteract their obsessions. These compulsions can be time-consuming and can lead to overthinking. On the other hand, overthinking itself is not a compulsion, but it can be a symptom of OCD.

Impairment

The overthinking symptom itself doesn't cause significant impairment in social, occupational, or other areas of life, but OCD can cause significant impairment in those areas.

Treatment

Overthinking can be treated with cognitive-behavioral therapy and mindfulness-based interventions. OCD, on the other hand, is treated with a combination of medications and cognitive-behavioral therapy (CBT) specifically designed for OCD.

Overthinking, Obsessing, and Overanalyzing

A Short Message from the Author

Hi, are you enjoying the book thus far? I'd love to hear your thoughts! Many readers do not know how hard reviews are to come by, and how much they help an author.

I would be incredibly thankful if you could take just 60 seconds to write a brief review, even if it's just a few sentences!

Thank you for taking the time to share your thoughts!

Chapter 5: The Neural Basis of Overthinking

Overthinking refers to the act of dwelling on a thought or situation for an excessive amount of time, to the point that it interferes with the individual's ability to function in their daily life. Overthinking often involves analyzing a situation repeatedly without coming to a resolution or decision.

Brain and Overthinking

When overthinking something, you're engaging in a lot of mental activity that doesn't impact the problem at hand. The brain is complex and interesting, but there are two major parts for thinking: the prefrontal cortex and the amygdala.

The prefrontal cortex is responsible for higher-level thinking, like planning and problem-solving. The amygdala is responsible for emotions—like fear and anxiety—and plays a role in memory formation. The two work together to predict what will happen in the future so they can prepare you for it.

When overthinking something, your brain gets stuck on one thing: how bad things could be if things don't go well. This makes sense! Your brain wants to keep you safe by telling you what might go wrong so that it can prepare you for whatever happens next. But sometimes, people take this worry too far, which means they spend way too much time trying to predict every possible outcome of their actions (even if those actions are reasonable).

Neurotransmitters and Overthinking

Neurotransmitters are chemical messengers that help your brain send signals throughout your body. Neurons or nerve cells release them, and they can travel across small gaps called synapses to reach other neurons.

Dopamine is a neurotransmitter that helps control the brain's reward and pleasure centers. Overthinking is often associated with an imbalance of dopamine and another important neurotransmitter called norepinephrine. Serotonin is another common neurotransmitter involved in overthinking. Serotonin helps regulate feelings of happiness, sadness, and anger. When serotonin levels are too low, it can lead to depression—a feeling of emptiness or sadness that can make you feel like nothing matters anymore.

When these chemicals start being released at higher than normal levels or are released more frequently than usual, it can cause some people to feel like their thoughts are racing out of control—and this can cause them to overthink things even further!

DMN and Overthinking

The default mode network (DMN) is a network of active brain regions that functions when we're not concentrating on anything in particular. It's involved in daydreaming, self-reflection, and introspection. This state of mind is often referred to as "the zone".

Overthinking is the opposite of using the DMN—it's an active condition where we are thinking about something that isn't happening right now. Overthinking can be useful for problem-solving and planning, but it can also affect our emotional health.

The first step towards overcoming overthinking is understanding how it works.

Overthinking is the opposite of the default mode and it means that you're so focused on one thing that everything else in your life fades into the background. When you're overthinking about something, likely, your DMN is not working properly—you've turned off your brain's passive state and taken control of every aspect of your life.

This can be harmful for several reasons. First, we need periods when we aren't thinking about anything at all—just letting our minds wander freely and not forcing ourselves to focus on anything specific. When we don't give those periods enough time, it becomes incredibly difficult to switch back into an active state of mind when we need to be productive or focused.

In addition, if you find yourself constantly worrying or stressing out about things that haven't happened yet (and therefore can't be controlled), then your brain will become overwhelmed by negative thoughts and emotions.

It's important to note that more research is needed to understand the precise relationship between overthinking and DMN and how it can be modulated; however, the current understanding is that DMN may be overactive in individuals who overthink can lead to repetitive and negative thoughts.

Stress and Trauma's Impact on Overthinking

Stress and trauma can have a significant impact on brain function and can contribute to overthinking.

Chronic stress and trauma can lead to changes in the brain, including alterations in the levels of neurotransmitters and hormones, as well as structural changes in brain regions such as the hippocampus, which is involved in memory and emotional regulation. These changes can lead to an overactive stress response, which can contribute to overthinking and other negative mental health outcomes.

Stress and trauma can also lead to negative thought patterns and emotional regulation difficulties, contributing to overthinking. For example, individuals who have experienced trauma may have difficulty controlling their thoughts and may ruminate on negative memories or experiences. This can lead to overthinking and difficulty shifting attention away from negative thoughts.

Additionally, stress and trauma can change how the brain processes information, leading to a heightened state of arousal and greater sensitivity to stressors, which can contribute to overthinking.

It's important to note that the impact of stress and trauma on brain function can vary depending on the individual and the nature of the stressor or trauma. It's also important to remember that overthinking is often a symptom of an underlying condition, and it's essential to address and manage it.

MINDFULNESS AND OTHER INTERVENTIONS

Practicing mindfulness and other interventions can change neural pathways and reduce overthinking by promoting brain chemistry and structure changes.

Mindfulness, cognitive-behavioral therapy (CBT), and mindfulness-based stress reduction (MBSR), have all been shown to alter the activity and connectivity of brain regions involved in emotional regulation, cognitive control, and attention, such as the prefrontal cortex, anterior cingulate cortex, and insula. These changes can lead to an increased ability to manage emotions, regulate attention, and shift perspective, which can reduce overthinking.

Research has also shown that mindfulness and other interventions can promote changes in the levels of neurotransmitters such as dopamine and serotonin, which play a role in regulating mood and motivation. These changes can lead to an improvement in mood and a decrease in anxiety and depression, which can contribute to reducing overthinking.

Mindfulness and other interventions can also change how the brain processes information and how it responds to stressors. By promoting a state of relaxation and a non-judgmental attitude towards thoughts, individuals can learn to observe their thoughts without becoming overly engaged with them, which can reduce overthinking.

It's important to note that the effects of mindfulness and other interventions can vary depending on the individual and the specific intervention being used. It's also important to remember that overthinking is often a symptom of an underlying condition, and it's essential to address it first. Consulting with a mental health professional who can guide you on the most appropriate intervention for your specific case is often recommended.

… Overthinking, Obsessing, and Overanalyzing

Chapter 6: Overcoming Overthinking

Overthinking is a huge problem for many people and can lead to anxiety, stress, and other negative emotions. However, overcoming it is possible by changing your mindset and focusing on what you CAN control.

Strategies

Overthinking is one of the most challenging things to manage, and it can be a real struggle to overcome.

However, it's not impossible—we've got some strategies for you!

1) Mindfulness meditation

2) Cognitive behavioral therapy

3) Talking through your thoughts with a friend or therapist

Mindfulness and Overthinking

Mindfulness is a great way to break the cycle of overthinking. It is a practice that helps you focus on the present moment instead of ruminating on past events or worrying about what might happen. It's about getting in touch with your body and surroundings and getting out of your head.

Overthinking is a common problem for many people, especially those prone to anxiety and depression. When we overthink, our brains constantly spin up scenarios that we can't control—and that gets exhausting! When you're mindful, you can focus on one thing at a time without jumping around like this.

Being mindful also helps us better understand our emotions and reactions to things. When we can pay attention to our bodies and thoughts, it becomes easier for us to notice when we're having an emotional reaction or feeling sad or stressed out. This awareness can help us decide how we want to respond in any given situation—and ultimately make life less overwhelming!

Mindfulness techniques and overthinking

We can all be mindful. It's just a matter of knowing what to do with that power. If you're like me, your mind is always going—even when you don't want it to be. However, there are some great techniques for training yourself to be more aware of the present moment rather than letting your thoughts pull you away from it.

Mindfulness techniques can help us manage our thoughts by teaching us how to notice them as they happen rather than letting them float through our minds without being recognized for what they are –

thoughts, not reality.

Here are some mindfulness techniques you might like to practice.

1) Take a few deep breaths as soon as you wake up in the morning (or before bed at night). This will help calm your mind, allowing you to focus on your breathing instead of all the other things around you (like emails or news alerts).

2) When you're feeling stressed or anxious about something, take a few minutes to just sit quietly in a chair by yourself with nothing else going on (no music playing, either). Focus on your breath while doing this and try not to think about anything else--just focus on how good having nothing else on your mind feels.

CBT AND OVERTHINKING

Cognitive-behavioral therapy (CBT) is a type of psychotherapy that helps people challenge and change negative thinking patterns. It's a short-term therapy that can help people cope with stress, anxiety, depression, and other mental health issues. The goal of CBT is to help people learn how to deal with thoughts and situations more positively so they can feel better.

CBT involves working with a trained therapist who will help you start recognizing the thoughts causing you problems. You'll learn how to challenge those thoughts and replace them with more positive ones. The therapist might also teach you different ways to respond when things go wrong—for example, if someone does or says something that upsets you, how can you respond instead of reacting negatively? By focusing on these kinds of situations and learning how to react differently, CBT helps people develop healthier responses that may lead them toward better mental health overall.

CBT Techniques

Cognitive-behavioral therapy (CBT) is a type of therapy that is based on the idea that our thoughts, feelings, and behaviors are interconnected. CBT can be an effective intervention for reducing overthinking and other mental health issues.

Here are some CBT techniques that you might like to try.

Identifying and challenging negative thoughts

The first step in CBT is identifying negative thoughts contributing to overthinking. Once identified, you can challenge these thoughts by questioning their validity and looking for evidence that contradicts them.

Reframing thoughts

Reframing is the process of looking at a situation in a different way. This can involve finding the positive aspects of a situation or looking at things from a different perspective.

Behavioral experiments

Behavioral experiments involve testing the validity of negative thoughts by gathering evidence through observation and experimentation. This can involve testing out different behaviors or thoughts to see how they impact your mood or behavior.

Mindfulness

Mindfulness is the practice of being present in the

moment and paying attention to your thoughts, feelings, and surroundings without judgment. Mindfulness can help to reduce overthinking by promoting a state of relaxation and a non-judgmental attitude towards thoughts.

Problem-solving

Problem-solving is a technique that helps to identify and solve problems that contribute to overthinking. This can involve breaking down a problem into smaller parts, generating possible solutions, and evaluating the pros and cons of each solution.

It's important to remember that CBT techniques are not a one-size-fits-all solution and that different techniques may work better for different individuals. It's best to work with a therapist who can help you develop a personalized treatment plan and guide you through learning and practicing these techniques.

SELF-CARE AND OVERTHINKING

Self-care is essential to maintaining good mental and physical health and can help reduce overthinking.

Here are some tips and advice for self-care.

Exercise

Regular physical activity has been shown to positively impact mental health, including reducing symptoms of anxiety and depression. Exercise releases endorphins, which are chemicals in the brain that act as natural painkillers and mood elevators. Aim for at least 30 minutes of moderate-intensity exercise most days of the week.

Healthy Eating

A balanced diet that includes fruits, vegetables, whole grains, and lean proteins can help support overall health and well-being. Avoiding processed foods, caffeine, and alcohol can also help to reduce symptoms of anxiety and depression.

Sleep

Getting enough sleep is essential for good physical and mental health. Aim for 7-9 hours of sleep each night and maintain a consistent sleep schedule.

STRESS MANAGEMENT

Finding ways to manage stress is essential for reducing overthinking. This can include techniques such as mindfulness, meditation, yoga, deep breathing, and progressive muscle relaxation.

SET BOUNDARIES

It's important to set boundaries for yourself and say *no* to things that don't serve you well. This can help to reduce stress and prevent burnout.

SEEK SUPPORT

Talking to friends, family, or a therapist can help you process your thoughts and feelings and provide a sounding board for your concerns.

ENGAGE IN ACTIVITIES YOU ENJOY

Engaging in activities you enjoy, such as reading, listening to music, painting, and cooking can help to reduce stress and improve your overall well-being.

It's important to remember that self-care is a journey,

and everyone's needs are different, so it's important to experiment and find what works best for you. It's also important to keep in mind that overthinking is often a symptom of an underlying condition, and it's essential to address the underlying condition first. Consulting with a mental health professional who can guide you on the most appropriate intervention for your specific case is often recommended.

Action Plan for Overthinking

Identify triggers

Make a list of situations or thoughts that tend to trigger excessive or unproductive overthinking.

Challenge negative thoughts

When you find yourself overthinking, try to challenge and reframe negative thoughts. Ask yourself if they are realistic and if the evidence supports them.

Practice mindfulness

Try to focus on the present moment and engage in

activities that help you stay present, such as meditation, yoga, or deep breathing exercises.

Limit Rumination

Try to limit the time you spend ruminating on a problem or thought by setting a timer for a specific amount of time, then redirecting your attention to something else.

Get Active

Engaging in physical activity, such as walking or running, can help reduce stress and distract you from overthinking. It also helps you to be present in the moment as you focus on your body's movements.

Seek Support

Talk to a therapist or counselor about your overthinking, as they can help you to develop coping strategies and improve your overall mental well-being.

Stay Organized

Keep a journal of your thoughts and feelings, and list

to-do items or tasks that need to be done.

Take a break

Permit yourself to take a break from certain tasks or problems and return to them later with a fresh perspective.

Keep a positive outlook

Try to focus on the positive aspects of your life and maintain a positive outlook.

Reward yourself

Reward yourself when you have successfully managed to control overthinking; this will help you focus on your progress and maintain a positive attitude toward your journey.

Support from Family and Professionals

Seeking support from friends, family, and

professionals is important when trying to manage overthinking. It can be a sign of an underlying mental health condition, such as anxiety or depression, and seeking professional help is often necessary to address the underlying issue and manage the symptoms of overthinking.

Friends and family can provide a supportive and understanding environment, and talking to them about your thoughts and feelings can help you process them and provide a sounding board for your concerns. They can also help you identify negative thought patterns and give you a different perspective on a situation.

Working with a therapist or counselor can also be beneficial in managing overthinking. A therapist can help you to identify the underlying causes of your overthinking and develop a personalized treatment plan to manage it. They can also teach you CBT techniques and other evidence-based strategies for managing overthinking and other mental health issues.

It's important to remember that seeking support is not a sign of weakness, and taking the first step toward recovery is essential. Friends and family can provide emotional support, but a mental health professional can provide the guidance and tools you need to manage overthinking and other mental health concerns.

In some cases, medication may also be recommended by a mental health professional as an adjunctive treatment along with the therapy. It's important to work with a medical professional to determine the best course of treatment for you.

Chapter 7: Supporting Loved Ones

Suppose you're a loved one of someone with OCD. In that case, you may be familiar with this scenario: You're sitting around the dinner table, and the person you care about suddenly says, "I'm worried that if I don't check the oven three times in the next two minutes, our entire apartment is going to catch on fire". Or maybe it's a text message: "I just had an intrusive thought about my parents dying in a car crash. Should I call them?"

It can be hard to know how to respond when obsessive thoughts and compulsive behaviors consume your loved one, but it's important to remember that these are real experiences for them—not just symptoms of some mental illness. The best thing you can do is be there for them, listen carefully, and show that you care.

We know it's hard to see someone you love deal with anxiety, but it's not always easy to understand what they're going through. It can be difficult to see someone you care about suffering from OCD and overthinking. While we can't imagine how difficult it must be for them, there is a lot we can do to help our loved ones feel supported during this time.

First off, don't dismiss their feelings! Be patient with them and try not to get frustrated when they're struggling with an obsession or compulsion. It's so important to remember that what your loved one is experiencing is real and valid—and you need to acknowledge that.

Next, listen! Just because you don't experience something doesn't mean it doesn't matter—and if your loved one has OCD or overthinking, then their thoughts are probably very important to them. When talking about their obsessions and compulsions, try not to interrupt them or tell them what they should focus on instead (even if the thought seems silly or trivial). Remember that when people are talking about something they're struggling with, they really just want someone who will listen without judgment.

Finally, offer support.

Tips for Supporting Loved Ones with OCD

When trying to help someone suffering from obsessive-compulsive disorder (OCD), it can be hard to know if you're doing the right thing. It's easy to get bogged down in the details, and it can be difficult to know where to start. Here are some tips for helping a loved one with OCD.

1. Don't be afraid to talk about it openly. The more you talk about your loved one's OCD, the better off they'll be—and the more comfortable you'll feel talking about it.

2. Don't try to fix their thoughts or behaviors for them; instead, offer support and encouragement as they work through this process themselves.

3. Listen carefully when your loved one is describing their symptoms, then let them know that you understand what they're going through by sharing something personal from your own experience or life story that relates directly back to what they're saying (e.g., "I know exactly how that feels because when I was young, I used to get anxious thinking about my death all the time").

4. Encourage them to see a therapist or counselor who specializes in OCD treatment (sometimes called "cognitive-behavioral therapy"). This can really help! It helps your friend or family member learn how to change their thoughts and behaviors to manage their symptoms better.

5. Offer practical support—if something specific is stressing them out (like an upcoming event), offer to help get everything together, so they don't have as much on their plate leading up to the event!

How Can You Support Your Loved Ones?

If a loved one is struggling with overthinking or obsessive-compulsive disorder (OCD), there are a few things you can do to support them.

Educate yourself about the condition. It can be helpful to understand what your loved one is going through so that you can better support them.

Be a good listener. Encourage your loved one to talk about their thoughts and feelings. Listen without judgment and try to understand their perspective.

Help them find professional help. OCD is a treatable condition, and professional help can make a big difference. Encourage your loved one to see a therapist or counselor specializing in OCD.

Help them stick to their treatment plan. Your loved one may be prescribed medication or therapy to help manage their symptoms. Help them stay on track with their treatment plan by reminding them of appointments or helping them take their medication as prescribed.

Practice self-care. It can be stressful to support a loved one who is struggling with OCD or overthinking. Make sure you're taking care of yourself too and finding healthy ways to cope with stress.

Be patient. Recovery from OCD can take time, and it's important to be patient and understanding with your loved one.

It's important to remember that everyone's experience with OCD is different and that respecting your loved one's boundaries and needs is important.

How Can You Take Care of Yourself?

Supporting a loved one with OCD or overthinking can be challenging, but there are steps to help them and take care of yourself.

Setting boundaries: It's important to set boundaries for yourself to avoid burnout. This can include setting limits on the amount of time and energy you can give to your loved one, as well as the types of conversations or behaviors you are comfortable with.

Avoiding burnout: Supporting a loved one with OCD or overthinking can be emotionally taxing. Make sure to take care of yourself by practicing self-care, such as exercising, eating healthily, and practicing stress management techniques.

Finding support: It can be helpful to talk to someone about your experience of supporting a loved one with OCD or overthinking. You can seek support from a therapist or counselor or talk to others who have had similar experiences.

Seeking professional help: If your loved one's condition is affecting your own mental health, it's important to seek help from a professional. A therapist or counselor can help you manage the stress and emotional toll of supporting a loved one with OCD or overthinking.

Helping your loved one seek professional help: Encourage your loved one to seek professional help, and if they are hesitant, offer to go with them to appointments or help them research therapists.

Be patient and understanding: Remember that recovery from OCD or overthinking can be a long process, and be patient with your loved ones as they work through it.

It's important to remember that everyone's experience with OCD or overthinking is unique and that respecting your loved one's boundaries and needs is important.

Conclusion

In conclusion, OCD and overthinking can have a profound impact on our daily lives, affecting our relationships, work, and overall well-being. These conditions can be overwhelming, isolating, and exhausting, but with the right support and treatment, it is possible to manage symptoms and improve our quality of life.

Throughout this book, we have explored the complexities of OCD and overthinking, including their causes, symptoms, and impact. We have discussed the various treatment options available, including medications, therapy, and self-help techniques.

Additionally, we have examined the overlap between OCD and overthinking and how these conditions can influence each other.

It is important to remember that seeking help for mental health concerns is not a sign of weakness, but rather a brave and necessary step towards healing. If you are struggling with OCD or overthinking, know that you are not alone, and there is always hope for recovery.

One of the key takeaways from this book is the importance of early intervention and seeking support from mental health professionals. With timely and effective treatment, many people with OCD and overthinking can successfully manage their symptoms and lead fulfilling lives. Remember that you are not alone in your journey. Reach out to family and friends for support, and consider joining a support group for people with OCD. Don't hesitate to seek professional help from a therapist or counselor who is trained in treating OCD. Together, with the help of professionals and loved ones, you can learn to manage your symptoms and take back control of your life.

In addition to professional support, there are also many self-help techniques and coping skills that can be effective in managing symptoms. These may include mindfulness-based interventions, stress management techniques, organizational and time-management strategies, and self-care practices.

Everyone's experience with OCD is unique, and what works for one person may not work for another. It may take some time to find the right combination of strategies and resources that work for you. But don't give up hope, as with time and persistence, you can learn to manage your symptoms and improve your quality of life.

It is also important to recognize the impact of OCD and overthinking on our loved ones, and to seek support from them when needed. In this book, we have discussed practical tips for supporting loved ones with OCD and overthinking, as well as strategies for taking care of ourselves while supporting others.

As we conclude this book, I want to reiterate my hope that it has provided a comprehensive resource for individuals struggling with OCD and overthinking, as well as their families and friends. I believe that by reading this book, you have gained a deeper understanding of these conditions, and feel empowered to take steps towards improving your mental health and overall well-being.

Remember, recovery from OCD and overthinking is a journey, and it may not always be easy. But with the right support and a commitment to your well-being, it is possible to achieve a brighter, more fulfilling future. I wish you all the best on your journey towards recovery, and encourage you to never give up hope.

As you finish reading this book, I encourage you to take action towards managing your OCD or overthinking symptoms. Whether it's seeking professional help, practicing self-care and coping strategies, or opening up to your loved ones about your struggles, taking that first step towards healing is essential.

It can be challenging to acknowledge that you are struggling with OCD or overthinking, but remember that seeking help is a sign of strength, not weakness.

You deserve to live a fulfilling life, free from the limitations and burdens of these conditions.

One effective way to take action is to set goals for yourself. What do you hope to achieve in managing your symptoms? Perhaps it's learning how to reduce the impact of intrusive thoughts, or practicing self-care techniques to reduce anxiety and stress. Whatever your goals may be, write them down and commit to taking small steps each day towards achieving them.

Another way to take action is to seek support from those around you. Whether it's opening up to a trusted friend or family member, or joining a support group, having a support system can make all the difference in managing your symptoms.

Finally, remember to celebrate your progress along the way. Healing is not always a linear process, and setbacks may occur. But by acknowledging and celebrating the progress you have made, you can build momentum and motivation towards achieving your goals.

In closing, I want to emphasize that recovery from OCD and overthinking is possible, and it begins with taking that first step towards healing. I encourage you to be gentle with yourself, take action towards your goals, and seek support when needed. You are not alone in your struggles, and there is always hope for a brighter future.

Thank you for reading!

Overthinking, Obsessing, and Overanalyzing

ONE MORE THING!

If you enjoyed this book and found it helpful, I'd be very grateful if you'd post a short review on Amazon. Your support does make a difference, and I read all the reviews personally so I can get your feedback and make this book even better. I love hearing from my readers, and I'd really appreciate it if you leave your honest feedback.

Thank you for reading!

BONUS CHAPTER

I would like to share a sneak peek into another one of my books that I think you will enjoy. The book is titled **_"How to Deal with Stress, Depression, and Anxiety: A Vital Guide on How to Deal with Nerves and Coping with Stress, Pain, OCD, and Trauma."_**

Are you tired of wasting your time and energy worrying all the time? Do you see the irrationality of constant worrying, but you can't seem to stop doing it? Are you ready to learn how to deal with anxiety and depression without taking drugs?

This book will walk you through precisely why, how, and what you need to do to stop worrying and start living your life.

Nearly 800 million people worldwide experience mental illness. Some of the most prominent adverse mental conditions include stress, anxiety, and depression. These issues can affect your psychological and physical health, and when you let them go untreated, they can have longstanding effects on your life and relationships. The more you ignore your mental strife, the harder it becomes to be resilient in the face of hardship, and if you let emotions get out of hand, they can lead to increased mental illness.

Though stress is an inseparable part of our lives, we can easily manage it using simple strategies and techniques. All we need is the willingness to learn these techniques and the ability to take action. Effective stress management is critical to your physical, psychological, and emotional health. It's vital to your overall well-being. This book will show you how to start managing your issues and get relief immediately.

How to Deal with Stress, Depression, and Anxiety provides a complete framework and a well-rounded set of tools to understand the causes of stress, depression, anxiety and how to overcome it.

Enjoy this free chapter!

Virtually all people experience stress, anxiety, or depression at various points in their lives. One 2017 study suggested that about 792 million people worldwide have formal mental health disorders, with depression and anxiety being the most common conditions. Millions, maybe even billions, of additional people experience subclinical conditions and high levels of stress, so the number of people who deal daily with such issues is quite astounding. When you live with any of these conditions, everyday activities become a challenge, and you may resort to self-sabotaging behaviors, or you feel stuck in place.

As these conditions continue, it only makes you feel worse, both mentally and physically. In the United States, it's been reported that stress affects the mental health of 73 percent of the population, leading to worsening conditions like depression and anxiety. While these conditions are all too common, they don't have to be. Living with mental illness or stress can feel impossible, and that's a hard burden to carry, which is why mental distress often leads to further mental and emotional anguish.

The Challenge

With so much external pressure in today's society to be their best selves, millions of people worldwide struggle to maintain their mental health and professional or personal well-being. Many emotionally and physically harmful behaviors—such as overworking and extreme self-sacrifice—are glorified by society. As people are pushed to do their best work and make room for a personal and social life, they can become consumed by anxiety and worries that impede their progress.

The statistics on stress, anxiety, and depression depict a grim picture. As the most prevalent mental health issue in the United States, according to the Anxiety and Depression Association of America, anxiety impacts over 40 million American adults, representing over 18 percent of the population. Globally, nearly 300 million people have anxiety. People who have anxiety tend to have greater stress levels, and 50 percent of those diagnosed with anxiety will also be diagnosed with depression. Depression rates are also startlingly high, with just under seven percent of the population experiencing major depression at any given time and another two percent experiencing persistent depressive disorder, also known as dysthymia or chronic depression.

Even if you don't have a clinically diagnosed issue, such as depression or anxiety, you likely have some degree of stress that makes it harder to function as you'd like to. The Global Organization for Stress says that 75 percent of people are moderately stressed, and nearly all people experience stress at some point in their lives because of a myriad of contributing factors. With so much mental dysfunction, it's no wonder that some people think they'll never get better, but this grim picture doesn't have to be your reality.

While mental health conditions have the power to destroy and debilitate people—paralyzing them and making it hard to have hope for the future— there are proven techniques anyone can use to improve their mental health and allow greater opportunity for personal development. You do not need to let your stress, anxiety, or depression hold you back anymore.

The solution to managing your mental health isn't easy or quick, but it is effective. With effort and careful attention to a multi-faceted plan, you can make dramatic improvements to your damaged mental health and start investing more energy into things that make you the most gratified. There are several steps you must follow for the best results. When you apply these steps, you can have increased mental clarity, emotional freedom, and confidence. Curing your mental health issues will require you to face everything that scares you and to admit uncomfortable truths. Still, you'll be far better off when you seek help than the nearly 25 million Americans who have untreated mental health conditions. You may not need the same level of care as people with more severe conditions, but you do need help because living with any degree of stress, anxiety, or depression is living with more pain than you need to have.

Treating a mental illness can seem intimidating to many people, but there are several effective methods, and there are ways to treat, if not cure, any mental health condition you may have. With so many adults and children not currently being treated for their mental health issues, it's no wonder that mental health statistics remain so prevalent. Still, with increased awareness and the greater availability of mental health resources, the prognosis for those who have mental illness continues to improve. Alongside this, as these issues become more widely acknowledged and discussed, the stigmas attached to them are beginning to dissipate, which removes some of the shame linked to mental illness, which only exacerbates it. Accordingly, by committing bravely to treatment and opening yourself to increased understanding of mental illness, you create resilience against mental illness and become more proactive in the treatment of these debilitating conditions.

For those of you with any of these issues, you cannot delay treatment. Mental dysfunction of any kind makes it harder to feel joy and, in the worst cases, it can deprive you of your ability to function. More than that, your mental health can also impact your physical health. For example, research has shown that stress increases the chance of someone dying from cancer by 32 percent. The Canadian Mental Health Association says that people with poor mental health are more prone to having chronic physical disorders.

A study from Johns Hopkins University found that patients with a family history of heart disease were healthier when they engaged in positive thinking. Among the participants of the study, those who had a positive outlook were 13 percent less likely to experience a cardiac event. Additionally, they found that, generally, people who have better outlooks live longer.

The Solution

Recovery is a process that isn't always linear, but this book will lay out the basic steps to help get you on the right track. The first step in the process is all about education. Before you can do anything else, you must understand the beast you're trying to slaughter and the sword you'll use to slay it. You'll learn how the brain works and how problems with its wiring can lead to mental dysfunction. You'll also learn how you can rewire your cognitive processes to promote increased mental health.

In the second step of the process, you'll continue your educational journey and gain a more in-depth understanding of what anxiety, stress, and depression are and how they impact the way you function. You'll start to understand how to address each of these issues using essential coping tools.

Once you've learned about each condition, you'll be introduced to one of the most powerful psychological tools for improved mental health: Cognitive Behavioral Therapy (CBT). You'll discover what CBT is and how to use it to address your mental ailments.

Once you understand the founding principles of these conditions and the fundamentals of CBT, you'll learn how to manage your circumstances daily by overcoming roadblocks and reviving your sense of self by shifting your perspective as you begin to think in new ways. You'll start to care for both your body and your mind in life-changing ways. All of these steps will lead to mental clarity and mental liberation.

With all this in mind, it's clear that a person's mental health impacts every part of their life, and without addressing your mental dysfunction, you'll never have the peace of mind you crave. Each day you do nothing about your mental health is another day you deprive yourself of health and happiness. Your mental health should be your priority, because you cannot fully function as a member of society if you're prohibited from doing all the things you love the most.

If you feel like you are losing sight of yourself and your desires because of your stress, anxiety, or depression, it's time to make a change. It's okay to be nervous about the adjustments you will need to make to feel healthier, but remember that being uncomfortable and uncertain is vital because they represent change. If you don't change, you'll never feel better than you do now. Maybe you have learned to live with your pain and worry, but it's time to learn to live without those negative coping mechanisms because they stop you from living your life to the fullest.

While the techniques in this book can help you improve your levels of stress, anxiety, and depression, I recommend seeking professional support to help push you towards your goals.

There are tons of books on this subject on the market, so thank you for choosing this one! "How to Deal with

Stress, Depression, and Anxiety" will provide a complete framework and a well-rounded set of tools for you to understand the causes of stress, depression, anxiety and how to overcome it. Please enjoy!

How Your Brain Works

Too many people hurt their recovery journey by working against their minds. They think they can force their brains into submission, and when that doesn't work, they feel like failures. When a change you're trying to make doesn't stick, it is usually because it isn't one your brain is used to. As much as you may want that change, your brain will resist it because unfamiliar things feel unsafe to the human brain. The human brain loves patterns, and it uses those patterns to create your internal mental programming and perceptions of reality. When you understand how your brain works, you can use it to your advantage to create new patterns and reframe your mental state.

Your brain is a powerful force, and it can work in remarkable ways. In facing your worries, doubts, and other negative feelings, you need to understand how your brain functions so you can stop fighting your brain and start working with it.

Your Map of Reality

In 1931, scientist and philosopher Alfred Korzybski

established an important metaphorical notion with his statement, "The map is not the territory." He believed that individuals don't have absolute knowledge of reality; instead, they have a set of beliefs built up over time that influence how they perceive events and situations. People's beliefs and views (their map) are not reality itself (the territory). In other words, perception is not reality.

Your brain fills gaps in understanding automatically. This means that when you don't know something, you subconsciously make an estimation based on the information you do know. When you experience worry or sadness, this can be caused by a map of reality that reinforces those ideas. That worry or sadness lingers in your mind and can shape future decisions unless you reshape your perception. Your map of reality will always be an interpretation, but it can be an interpretation that helps you rather than hurts you. You can change your map of reality and make it more productive by addressing your thoughts and beliefs and how they impact your behavior.

Thoughts, Core Beliefs, and Behavior

Beliefs are sets of ideas that individuals use to dictate how they'll behave. A belief is something you think is a fact. You feel so strongly about something that you're almost positive it's true, regardless of how well you can prove it. You may have some doubts from time to time, but, overall, you consistently stick to those beliefs. Beliefs are attitudes that you fall back on, because they provide a sense of security, and they make you feel that certain things are constant, which is why something that makes you doubt your beliefs can be so painful. Your beliefs drive your unconscious, habitual behaviors. They become so ingrained in you that they feel natural and inherently true.

When you have trouble managing situations or coping with feelings, you automatically turn to your beliefs for help without exerting too much brainpower. Your beliefs help you determine morality, and they help you decide whether people or things are bad or good. Your whole perspective uses a compilation of your beliefs to fill in the parts of your reality you can't fully understand.

Beliefs are formed based on past experiences and the stimuli around us. Most people's core beliefs—the most driving beliefs they have—are established when they're young children. As they grow older, children commonly challenge the beliefs they've been taught as they begin to think more critically and independently. Nevertheless, many children reaffirm the beliefs they were taught rather than disproving them. As adults, they can challenge these beliefs and, by managing their beliefs, they can create a healthier view of the world that's a more realistic map of reality.

Beliefs can be incredibly powerful. For example, imagine parents telling their children that paperclips are dangerous. Telling a child that paperclips are dangerous seems silly. Nevertheless, when those words go unchallenged, the child will internalize the message, and they might try to avoid paperclips, which could impede their ability to do certain tasks. But as they grow older, the child would likely challenge that belief and overcome the fear of paperclips.

Other beliefs may be harder to debunk. For instance, if a mom tells her child that dogs are dangerous, the child may become afraid of dogs. This fear could continue into adulthood, because the child has learned to be terrified of dogs. Even rational arguments that dogs aren't something to be scared of may still make it hard for that child to believe. After all, dogs, unlike paperclips, do have the potential to bark and bite. The child would be so convinced by the belief that it would be hard for them to break from that mindset.

You may have beliefs that stand in your way and feel so foundational to who you are that challenging them makes you uncomfortable. Nevertheless, you need to contemplate your limiting beliefs.

While thoughts and beliefs may seem similar, there are some profound differences between them that you must acknowledge if you want to have a complete understanding of how your thoughts and beliefs can make or break your mental health. Thoughts help to form your beliefs. When you have the same thoughts repeatedly, they become beliefs. You become so used to the thoughts that they become ingrained in your subconscious, and it becomes hard to imagine that those thoughts aren't true. Accordingly, when you think negatively, you tend to have a more pessimistic outlook.

Not all thoughts are beliefs. The thoughts that come and go through your mind without repetition never become beliefs. Beliefs are a product of habitual thinking. This means that while it may be hard to break them, you can break them by overwriting those negative thoughts with positive ones, which is a practice that many therapies and techniques discussed in this book use to reduce stress, anxiety, and depression.

As you've seen with the map of reality, perception shapes our views, and it also shapes the way we think. Your thoughts build your beliefs, and your beliefs, in turn, build your sense of what's real. Some of your beliefs will empower you to seek success and find happiness, while others will make the world seem like a dark and scary place with no hope. Try to identify the parts of your belief system that cause you to have negative responses.

Your thought patterns have tremendous power to

change your life. The simple act of interrupting negative thought patterns can help you begin to make changes. These changes don't happen overnight, and deeply entrenched beliefs may even take months or years to debunk completely, but, when you focus on the thought patterns you want to instill, you start to question the "truths" you blindly believed.

There will be some beliefs you'll want to keep, and those are ones you can build upon and use to your advantage throughout this process. There's no need to get rid of any belief that's constructive because such beliefs are the ones that help you grow. However, be honest about the beliefs that are hurting you. Many people try to rationalize certain beliefs that they feel psychologically unready to call into question. Open your mind and contemplate, "Is this belief hurting me in covert and manipulative ways?" If you struggle even to pose that question about a particular belief, that belief may be a harmful one.

The way you think isn't something that's out of your control. According to the Massachusetts Institute of Technology (MIT), 45 percent of your daily choices are habitual, meaning they're a product of your subconscious thought patterns and beliefs. You choose what stimuli you feed to your subconscious. When worries or hopelessness begin to fill your head, try saying to yourself, "The world is a place full of opportunity and good things." While it won't feel like saying this is doing anything at first, rewriting your internal monologue can be a powerful first step toward growth.

When you understand how thoughts and core beliefs shape your behaviors, it becomes easier to create a path for growth. You learn that you're in charge of your beliefs, and your thoughts can only have as much control over you as you give them. You may feel helpless against your negative thoughts, but learning to overcome these harmful thoughts and release the power they have over you is the only way to become a happier person. The more you try to avoid the things that make you anxious, stressed, or depressed, the more anxious, stressed, and depressed you'll become.

Cognitive Distortions

While your brain does its best to give you helpful

information and create an accurate perception of reality, sometimes it gets a little lost trying to translate what it observes into a sensible perception. Your brain loves to make connections, and sometimes, it will make connections that are overly simplified and don't show the nuance in a situation. This is called a cognitive distortion.

Simple speaking, cognitive distortions are falsehoods that your brain persuades you into believing are true. Cognitive distortions can take a variety of forms, but one common example is polarized thinking. When you think in polarities, you see things as wrong or right, good or bad, or win or lose. After you fail at one task, you may start to think, "I'll fail every task because I can't do anything right." This perception isn't an accurate one, but you become convinced it's true because your brain has pinpointed what it thinks is a pattern.

The problem with cognitive distortions is that they're often shrouded in negativity. They make you expect the worse, and they convince you that you cannot do certain things or that other things are unsafe.

Cognitive distortions change your perspective, and they can quickly become harmful to your overall well-being. If you believe false messages, it's hard to make peace with your situation or feel secure. When you feel insecure, your mental health declines, and your doubts start to make it harder to function normally. Anxiety may take hold, and you may feel more stressed as you try to complete tasks. The hardship of your situation may then lead to depression.

Cognitive distortions can also cause you to act in ways that worsen your mental state. For example, someone with an eating disorder may tell themselves, "Not eating helps me," when they lose a couple of pounds. They keep going with harmful behaviors because a faulty pattern was established of believing that an action is "good," even though the behavior, for obvious reasons, is the opposite of helpful.

Likewise, someone with anxiety may say, "Avoiding this task will make me feel calmer," when procrastination only heaps on the pressure and stress of the situation. Delaying the task may have given them a sense of relief before, so they keep doing it. It continues to impair them, but cognitive distortion causes them to keep repeating the same harmful behavior. Cognitive distortions fool you into thinking certain actions are good for you or that they aren't as harmful as they are. Someone may engage in risky behavior and think, "This won't hurt me because it didn't harm me before," when that's not accurate information. People often use these distortions to justify harmful, habitual behaviors that give temporary relief to mental distress, but this causes more problems in the long run.

Negative Thoughts

Negative thoughts can play an influential role in how your brain works because your thoughts help create your map of reality and form your cognitive distortions. It's much easier to give in to negative thoughts than positive ones. People often expect the worst because they're afraid that having hope will lead to disappointment. Negative thoughts are also fueled by the internalization of negative comments that others have made about you in the past. For instance, if your mother tells you that you're ugly, you may start to think you're unattractive until it ultimately becomes a core belief.

Research has shown how much healthier and happier people are when they think positively because the brain responds to the input we give it. So, you can change your outlook by thinking with more positivity. When you think negatively, you're feeding your brain with information it can use against you; therefore, give it information that will help you instead!

THE ROLE OF TRAUMA

Trauma is a significant part of human life, and it can be one of the largest contributors to adverse mental health outcomes, including increased depression, anxiety, and stress. According to the National Council for Behavioral Health, 70 percent of adults in the United States have experienced at least one traumatic event, which means that 223.4 million people in the United States alone have had trauma. Moreover, among people who seek treatment for mental health issues, 90 percent have gone through trauma. Consequently, if you have trauma, it contributes to some of the issues you may be experiencing.

Trauma is the result of events that cause deep worry or distress. Traumatic experiences are often those that either threaten a person's life or the life or well-being of those they love.

You can have both physical and emotional trauma. Physical trauma can be a response to accidents, injuries, or other physical events. Physical trauma often can trigger emotional trauma, and the scars from emotional trauma often linger longer than those of physical trauma. Trauma can result from physical, verbal, emotional, or sexual abuse, and children who live in violent environments are at an increased risk for trauma. Some people don't realize they have trauma. They might say, "Oh, well, what I went through wasn't that bad compared to other people." However, trauma doesn't mean you were tortured or injured in unthinkable ways. The death of people you love or contracting a serious disease can also cause trauma. Anything can be traumatic if it makes you feel unsafe, so don't downplay those feelings—accept how you feel, even if you don't think it's "that bad."

When you have trauma that you haven't addressed,

you're bound to have increased mental challenges. Trauma alone doesn't lead to mental illness, but it's a major contributing factor, and it drives you to rely on unhealthy coping mechanisms that do you more harm than good.

Trauma changes the way you think, which can impact your decision-making processes and your unconscious thoughts. Trauma makes your brain feel unsafe, and when your brain feels unsafe, it focuses on protecting you from future pain, because that pain could threaten your survival. Even in circumstances that don't usually cause anxiety, you may start to feel threatened, even if you can't logically explain why. When you go through trauma, your brain has a stress response, and that stress response reacts to the trauma by changing your future behaviors in an attempt to protect you.

The stress response involves areas of the brain, including the prefrontal cortex, hippocampus, and amygdala. These areas experience lingering changes when they undergo the intense pressure of trauma. As a result, the way your brain processes information shifts when you experience trauma. Your amygdala becomes more active. This part of your brain is responsible for your flight-or-fight reactions and, when it's overactive, it can make you feel as though you're in danger in non-dangerous situations. It stays on guard because it wants to prevent any potential threats from sneaking up on you.

When your amygdala becomes more active, you may be more prone to feeling stressed, and the hippocampus—the part of your brain that handles short-term memories—may become less active. As a result, you may struggle to differentiate between things that happened to you in the past and things that are presently happening.

Finally, the pre-cortex may shrink, and when it does, you have trouble dealing with your emotions and regulating your thoughts. Many of these changes can be found in people who have post-traumatic stress disorder (PTSD), but anyone with trauma can experience them to a lesser degree.

For obvious reasons, trauma makes it hard for you to be mentally healthy, but it also makes it hard for you to be physically healthy. When your physical health declines, this creates additional causes of anxiety, stress, and depression. Thus, not only can your mental health make your physical health worse, but your physical health can make your mental health worse. The Canadian Mental Health Association reports that people with depression are three times as likely to have chronic pain than people without depression. People who have chronic pain are two times as likely to have anxiety or a mood disorder. Mental and physical health are often dependent on one another, which is why the correlations between the two are so important.

According to statistics, you are more likely to experience health issues such as chronic obstructive pulmonary disease (COPD), heart disease, high blood pressure, cancer, and diabetes when you have trauma. These conditions can all reduce your life's quality or longevity, which can then create even more mental unrest. That psychological turbulence can lead to your physical conditions worsening. You can see how these situations can quickly become bleak for those experiencing them. However, by addressing your trauma, you can reduce the potency of some of these issues.

Trauma, unfortunately, is a normal part of life. For many people, it's challenging to manage, but it's nothing to be ashamed of. Using the strategies in this book, you can learn to become conscious of your trauma and take away the power it has to control your life. Simple techniques like listening to music, establishing a healthy diet and exercise routine, practicing meditation, and admitting you have trauma are just some of the most basic techniques you can use to recover.

Recovery from trauma is painful, but it's one of the most important things you can do for your health because working through trauma allows you to heal your brain and teach it new patterns.

Get Professional Help

Before you do anything, you should seek professional help. Seeing a doctor or a mental health professional can help ensure that you have a support system in place to help you improve yourself.

While this book's techniques can help you improve your levels of stress, anxiety, and depression, some people will still need professional support to help push them toward their goals. Additionally, for some people, these issues may be related to their brain chemistry, which may require medication. To have a satisfactory recovery experience, you must take a holistic approach that ensures you achieve long-lasting results and can learn coping skills that will shape the rest of your life.

Get your full copy today! ***"How to Deal with Stress, Depression, and Anxiety: A Vital Guide on How to Deal with Nerves and Coping with Stress, Pain, OCD, and Trauma."***

BOOKS BY RICHARD BANKS

Assertiveness Training: Learn How to Say No and Stop People-Pleasing by Establishing Healthy Boundaries

The Keys to Being Brilliantly Confident and More Assertive: A Vital Guide to Enhancing Your Communication Skills, Getting Rid of Anxiety, and Building Assertiveness

The Art of Active Listening: How to Listen Effectively in 10 Simple Steps to Improve Relationships and Increase Productivity

How to Deal With Stress, Depression, and Anxiety: A Vital Guide on How to Deal with Nerves and Coping with Stress, Pain, OCD and Trauma

How to Deal with Grief, Loss, and Death: A Survivor's Guide to Coping with Pain and Trauma, and Learning to Live Again

Develop a Positive Mindset and Attract the Life of Your Dreams: Unleash Positive Thinking to Achieve Unbound Happiness, Health, and Success

How to Stop Being Negative, Angry, and Mean: Master Your Mind and Take Control of Your Life

For the Full Book Listing go to https://author.to/RichardBanksBooks

REFERENCES

"Obsessive-compulsive Disorder (OCD)." National Health Service. Retrieved from https://www.nhs.uk/mental-health/conditions/obsessive-compulsive-disorder-ocd/overview/

"Obsessive-compulsive Disorder." Mayo Clinic. Mayo Foundation for Medical Education and Research. Retrieved from https://www.mayoclinic.org/diseases-conditions/obsessive-compulsive-disorder/symptoms-causes/syc-20354432

"OCD-UK." OCD-UK. Retrieved from https://www.ocduk.org/

"Obsessive-compulsive Disorder (OCD)." Mind. Retrieved from https://www.mind.org.uk/information-support/types-of-mental-health-problems/obsessive-compulsive-disorder-ocd/about-ocd/

"About OCD." International OCD Foundation. Retrieved from https://iocdf.org/about-ocd/

"Obsessive-compulsive Disorder (OCD)." NHS Inform. Retrieved from https://www.nhsinform.scot/illnesses-and-conditions/mental-health/obsessive-compulsive-disorder-ocd

"What are the Social Signs of OCD?" Healthline. Retrieved from https://www.healthline.com/health/ocd/social-signs

"Intrusive thoughts in OCD: Symptoms and treatment." Gateway OCD. Retrieved from https://www.gatewayocd.com/intrusive-thoughts-ocd-symptoms-and-treatment/

"What are Common OCD Thoughts?" Verywell Mind. Retrieved from https://www.verywellmind.com/what-are-common-ocd-thoughts-2510680

"Different Types of OCD." TreatMyOCD. Retrieved from https://www.treatmyocd.com/education/different-types-of-ocd

"What Are the Different Types of OCD?" Self. Retrieved from https://www.self.com/story/ocd-types

"Intrusive Thoughts: Understanding, Coping, and Overcoming." Positive Psychology. Retrieved from https://positivepsychology.com/intrusive-thoughts/

"How to Know When You're Overthinking." Verywell Mind. Retrieved from https://www.verywellmind.com/how-to-know-when-youre-overthinking-5077069

"How to Stop Overthinking." Tony Robbins. Retrieved from https://www.tonyrobbins.com/mental-health/how-to-stop-overthinking/

"What Causes Overthinking and 6 Ways to Stop." Forbes. Retrieved from https://www.forbes.com/health/mind/what-causes-overthinking-and-6-ways-to-stop/

Made in the USA
Columbia, SC
20 January 2025